FORCE, FATE, AND FREEDOM

FORCE,
FATE,
and
FREEDOM

On Historical Sociology

Reinhard Bendix

UNIVERSITY OF CALIFORNIA PRESS

Berkeley, Los Angeles, London

University of California Press
Berkeley and Los Angeles, California

University of California Press, Ltd.
London, England

©1984 by
The Regents of the University of California

Printed in the United States of America

1 2 3 4 5 6 7 8 9

Library of Congress Cataloging in Publication Data

Bendix, Reinhard.
  Force, fate, and freedom.

  Includes bibliographical references.
  1. Liberty—Addresses, essays, lectures.
2. Rationalism—Addresses, essays, lectures. 3. Social
sciences—Philosophy—Addresses, essays, lectures.
4. History—Philosophy—Addresses, essays, lectures.
5.Weber, Max, 1864–1920—Addresses, essays, lectures.
I. Title.
HM271.B378   1983   300'.1   83-3565
ISBN 0-520-04931-4

Contents

Foreword

The University of Heidelberg established a Max Weber Guest Professorship at its Institute of Sociology in 1981. The purpose of this position is to cultivate scholarly communication at an international level, as well as to further important aspects of the university's own tradition. The name of Max Weber represents scholarly work of international standing. Weber also represents a broad, if heterogeneous movement of thought in the cultural and social sciences that is associated with Heidelberg. This movement began toward the end of the nineteenth century, and its repercussions continue to the present. The names of Wilhelm Windelband, Emil Lask, Heinrich Rickert, and Karl Jaspers are associated with the movement in philosophy. Also part of the group are leading scholars like Ernst Troeltsch in theology, Georg Jellinek and Gustav Radbruch in law, and Max and Alfred Weber, Eberhard Gothein, Emil Lederer, and the young Karl Mannheim in economics and sociology. An intellectual perspective arose from this scholarly constellation which is perhaps most clearly expressed in the work of Max Weber.

What characterizes this perspective? The answer lies in the tasks of the cultural and social sciences as Max Weber has outlined them. "Our aim is the understanding of the *characteristic uniqueness* of the reality in which we move. We wish to understand, on the one hand, the relationships and the *cultural significance* of individual events in their contemporary manifestations and, on the other, the causes of their being historically so and not otherwise."[1] For Weber this reality is in the first place the social and economic life of European and American civilization, which tends toward rationalism in specific ways. The main task of the cultural and social science disciplines, as he sees it, is to explain these tendencies toward rationality and to formulate concepts suitable to their analysis. Both the understanding of our particular reality and the explanation of its rationalizing tendencies presuppose, however, that we contrast these with other realities and that we avoid a reductionist analysis of their complexities, whether such reductionism has a materialistic or an idealistic bias. Weber's approach is, therefore, oriented toward a comparative analysis of ideas, interests, and institutions across different cultures and time periods. The purpose of such an analysis is to interpret the interrelations of different aspects of our "cultural life" that arise from the relations between structures of meaning and conditions of existence. The ultimate purpose of this approach is, to paraphrase a formulation from Weber's preface to his collected essays on the sociology of religion, to understand and explain the origin of the special character of Occidental culture and, within this broad theme, of the cultural life of modern Western civilization.[2]

The Max Weber Guest Professorship was inaugurated in the summer semester of 1981. In view of the significance of the occasion, a search was undertaken for a prominent scholar in the sociocultural sciences whose work is intimately related to Weber's. But the search was not difficult. The problem lay in persuading our candidate to accept: he was Reinhard Bendix, whose personal fate, in his own words, had caused him to become a builder of intellectual bridges between Germany and the United States.

The criterion of prominent scholarship is easily dealt with in a sketch of the career of Reinhard Bendix, whose continuous achievements have won worldwide academic recognition over the years. Following his forced emigration from Nazi Germany in

1938, his doctoral studies at the University of Chicago, and an interlude at the University of Colorado, Bendix settled at the University of California in Berkeley. He has taught there since 1947, with numerous intermezzi provided by research fellowships from major foundations and institutions, and visiting professorships in the United States and throughout the world, especially in Germany. Bendix was elected president of the American Sociological Association for 1969–70; from 1966 to 1970 he served as vice-president of the International Sociological Association; and in 1977 he was elected to the American Philosophical Society. Recently, his work has been specially recognized by honorary doctoral degrees awarded him at the University of Leeds (1978) and the University of Mannheim (1980).

The body of Bendix's work—including his first major comparative study, *Work and Authority in Industry,* which received the McIver Prize in 1958—now comprises several thousand pages, most of them translated into several languages, and all of them the product of an effort that only very few members of his generation have undertaken. Bendix has devoted himself to a calling which refuses to follow intellectual fashions, but which rather pursues an autonomous and clearly defined aim. He is indebted to a European tradition of comparative cultural and social history, as established above all by Karl Marx, Alexis de Tocqueville, Jacob Burckhardt, Max Weber, and Otto Hintze. In this regard, the work of Weber in particular has never become merely a superficial point of reference. On the contrary, it has exercised a profound formative impact on the intellectual core of Bendix's work. The result of this impact is an affinity which is illustrated in three aspects of Bendix's oeuvre: his contribution to the American reception of Max Weber's work; his incorporation of Weberian problems and concepts into his own research; and his use and advancement of the Weberian perspective on the basic issues of the sociocultural sciences and on the intellectual situation of our time.

Reinhard Bendix's contribution to the positive American reception of Weber's work is most clearly manifested in two books: *Max Weber: An Intellectual Portrait* and the essay collection written with Guenther Roth, *Scholarship and Partisanship.* The intellectual portrait of Weber has been Bendix's most successful publication. His main purpose therein was to introduce Weber's historical and empirical work to the American student with no knowledge of German. (This overview was published at a time when, for example, a complete English translation of *Economy and Society* was not yet available.) Of course, the remarkable effect the book has had is not merely the result of a happily chosen didactic purpose. It is also related to the intellectual underpinnings on which Bendix's account of Weber rests. Like the collection of essays, the *Portrait* can be understood not only as a scholarly work, but also as the statement of an intellectual position: theoretically in support of power, the conflict of interests, and legitimation in opposition to systemic equilibrium and consensus; methodologically in support of the historical analysis of constellations in opposition to a deductive analysis; and politically in support of a pluralistic world in opposition to American ethnocentrism.

With the *Portrait,* Bendix attempted to provide the American reader with a new access to Weber, a strategy that distinguished it from the comprehensive and systematic approach developed by Talcott Parsons.[3] For Parsons, Weber is part of an intellectual tradition, to be integrated on the basis of a systems theory. For Bendix, Weber's work projects a viable research program. For Parsons, America is the fulfillment of Europe. For Bendix, the political and cultural fate of Europe remains a persistent challenge to America. In this respect, Bendix—in contrast to some other German refugees—basically has embraced American political culture and its institutions. And yet Bendix's book confronts the American understanding of Weber with a European interpretation—not a naïve position by any means, but one that has been transmuted by the experience of emigration.

Viewed from this perspective, another aspect of the *Portrait* comes to light. In the wake of the experience of National Socialism, it represents "a bridge to German culture,"[4] perpetuating and advancing Bendix's own heritage in a quite different political and cultural setting. This holds true especially for the legacy of his father, who as a German Jew took the path of assimilation and identified himself with German culture and the German idea of the Rechtsstaat, a nation-state legitimated by its commitment to the rule of law. For one feature of the German legal tradition

that Bendix's father actively supported is incorporated into Max
Weber's sociology of law and of domination and is also employed
in his comparative historical analyses.

Thus it is no accident that this feature of Weber's work had a
profound influence on Bendix's own perspective. In the center of
this perspective lies the problem of domination, in the dual sense
of legitimation and organization. The problem of bureaucratization is intimately related to this issue because, to borrow Weber's
language, the exercise of domination requires not only a ruler,
but also an administrative staff. Although the problem of domination is an authentically Weberian issue, in Bendix's work it is
developed in a distinctive way. This is unquestionably related to
Bendix's own experience—indeed, the experience of his generation—for which the encounter with totalitarianism and authori-
tarianism was decisive. Against this background, Bendix read
Weber primarily as a political sociologist, and in his own historical work he was chiefly interested in the political dimension of
structures of social action. The collapse of the German Rechtsstaat and the disenfranchisement that this entailed for many, including Bendix, gave him a sensitivity to the objective predica-
ment and the subjective perceptions of the disenfranchised in
history. Perhaps that is why he never regarded disenfranchisement as a purely economic question, or even a purely cultural
problem, but always as a political issue.

Even the titles of Bendix's three main comparative studies
suggest his interest in a political history, interpreted in these
terms: *Work and Authority in Industry, Nation-Building and Citizenship,* and *Kings or People.* All these books undertake a comparative investigation of the institutionalization of domination
and the problems it produces, both for the distribution of power
and of life-chances, on one hand, and for the problems of meaning and of life goals, on the other. In the progression of these
three studies, the object of investigation becomes increasingly
complex, the regional scope more comprehensive, and the tem-
poral horizon more encompassing. In *Work and Authority in Industry,* the focal point is the individual enterprise and its locus in
the economic order of Russia and the West since the Industrial
Revolution. In *Nation-Building and Citizenship,* the focus is
broadened to the political order and the processes of transforma-

tion that began in Europe long before the Industrial Revolution, even long before the democratic revolutions. These processes are investigated, not only in the context of the societies of Eastern and Western Europe, but also in India and Japan. Finally, in *Kings or People*, the main issue is the relation between political order and cultural traditions, which produced historical legacies with a potential for legitimation whose origins must be sought in the Middle Ages. In this book, Bendix not only analyzes societies which had mastered the challenge of economic modernization relatively successfully, such as the Western European societies, Russia, and Japan. He also considers the developing nations and their quest for national identity within the constraints of an international economic system which is based fundamentally on their exploitation. Linking these three works is the attempt to develop a comparative analysis of transformational crises and of crises in the meaning and purpose of life. The ultimate aim of these studies is a universal history of uneven development.

The attempt to write this kind of universal history requires, above all, intensive historical research. It also demands a powerful formative imagination, for which the always precarious relation between the general and the particular represents a constant challenge. However, neither the commitment to the progress of knowledge nor the impulse toward a narrative analysis can account for the remarkable energy required to produce a book like *Kings or People*. A more profound interest is indispensable, one linked with the sort of understanding achieved by the sociocultural sciences and the aims to which they are committed. Especially in the contemporary phase of history (although our times do not constitute a world society, they certainly comprise a *single* world), the foundations of the sociocultural sciences should be laid in such a way that these disciplines can contribute to the development of an historical consciousness concerning the origins and distinctiveness of the world we live in. For this purpose, two maxims can be derived from European cultural and social science, and especially from the work of Max Weber: our analyses must be comparative, and they must also be structural-historical. It is above all these two maxims that Bendix has employed in his work. In this respect, he has resisted the predominant trend in our discipline for many years.

Comparative analyses, however, certainly do not seem irreconcilable with the dominant doctrine. Every scientific experiment rests on a comparison, which at the very least schools our ability to judge what ideas and institutions go together. However, causal explanation and the development of historical awareness are two different things. From Bendix's perspective, therefore, it is necessary to distinguish a trivial from a nontrivial sense of comparative analysis. The latter is concerned with the formulation of unrealized historical possibilities and alternative realities. When we neglect the comparative perspective in this sense, we are likely to commit the fallacy of retrospective determinism, or to regard our own sociocultural reality as the best of all possible worlds. Because of the heterogeneity of history, we are also inclined to employ concepts that are too broad, and to generalize prematurely. One can study the consequences of both pitfalls in evolutionism and neo-evolutionism. Seen in this light, comparative analysis is a weapon to be wielded against closed theories of history, as well as grand deductive theories.

A comparative sociology, of course, must also begin with universal questions, such as the problem of domination, and with such diachronic schemata as the juxtaposition of tradition and modernity. However, the interest of the comparative perspective does not lie in the universal problems, but rather in the various alternative solutions men have found to them. Moreover, the juxtaposition of tradition and modernity is a heuristic device for identifying concrete and variable relationships, such as those between pioneers and latecomers. Thus the primary aim of historical comparison is to work out alternative developmental tendencies and their results. This approach promotes an open conception of history, as well as middle-range concepts and generalizations that lie between what holds true for all societies and what holds true only for a single society.

Structural-historical analysis is also important for the development of historical awareness. By means of such analysis, attention is focused chiefly on the structural conditions of historical action. These extend from geographical, ecological, and economic to cultural conditions (historical legacies, for example). All these conditions influence the responses which historical actors can find to challenges such as economic modernization. Here, however, in contrast to certain versions of structuralism, the autonomous and immanent dynamic of the structures themselves is not presupposed. On the contrary, the scope of free action which was once available to historical actors, and which remains open to contemporary conduct, should be discovered. Insofar as actors exploit these opportunities, they make history. But they make history under preexisting, not autonomously chosen conditions. As a result, they become implicated on occasion in unintended—and thereby fateful and potentially tragic—consequences. To refuse simply to submit to both the conditions and their consequences, but rather to respond to them and hold oneself responsible: this is the stance encouraged by a structural-historical analysis. In this respect, such an analysis can be seen as a weapon against historical fatalism, focusing attention on our responsibility before history.

Historical legacies are not abstractions. They intervene more or less dramatically in our personal lives. They determine our group membership, and thus also the definition of our identity. When group membership comes into question, then doubts arise also about identity. Reinhard Bendix has experienced this fateful connection both through his father and in his own life, and his most recent book is devoted to clarifying it. Both were forced to leave Germany: under the Nazis, it was impossible as a Jew to be a German, even if one no longer wanted to be a Jew. Moreover, Bendix's image of history has been indelibly stamped by the consciousness of escaping the Holocaust by accident and also by the awareness that this accident entailed a further deprivation of identity. It is understandable that someone who has withstood, and come to terms with, such a life-threatening experience should construct a cosmopolitan identity and lead an intellectual existence between America and Europe. It is also understandable that he should regard world history as a way of overcoming both ethnocentrism and disorientation.

The Max Weber Lectures are the focal point of the Max Weber Guest Professorship. They do not have to be lectures on Weber, but they should be in the spirit of Weber. This describes the following chapters, which could be called reflections on a scholarly career committed to the Weberian heritage. Seen in this light, they can be read both as an introduction to Weber's research program and as an introduction to the life work of Rein-hard Bendix. Above all, they are a convincing and eloquent defense of the comparative and structural-historical perspective in political science and sociology.

Wolfgang Schluchter
Professor of Sociology
Heidelberg University

Preface

The six chapters of this book originated with the invitation by
Professor Wolfgang Schluchter, University of Heidelberg, to de-
liver the first series of public lectures in the newly established
Max Weber Guest Professorship at Heidelberg in the summer
semester 1981. I am indebted to Professor Schluchter not only for
the honor of the invitation, but for the cordial hospitality extended to my wife and me during our stay in Heidelberg, as well
as for the care with which he edited my German text. Finally, I
thank him for writing a foreword to this English edition, which I
have translated from the German.

The English version of this book is in fact the original, though
I have modified it in the light of improvements and elaborations
made in the German edition, which has already appeared under
the title *Freiheit und Historisches Schicksal* (Suhrkamp Verlag,
1982). My oral presentations were adapted to an hour-long for-
mat, but this book is unabbreviated. Three of the lectures were
presented as the Albion W. Small Lectures at the University of
Chicago, October 1982.

I am indebted to the Department of Political Science and to
the Administration of the University of California, Berkeley, for

the research leave which allowed me to prepare these chapters in their present form. I wish also to thank my colleagues Victoria Bonnell, Ernst Haas, Lynn Hunt, Gail Lapidus, Thomas Laqueur, and Ann Swidler for their comments on earlier drafts of the first two chapters.

Work and Authority in Industry (1956), *Nation-Building and Citizenship* (1964), and *Kings or People* (1978) are three separate studies with one theme: authority and the problem of legitimation. My analysis of this theme employs two sets of related concepts: ideas and interests, that is, the subjective meaning of human action and its relation to the structure of society. These themes and concepts play a central role in the work of Max Weber. I have used Weber's work as a source of inspiration for explorations of my own, and I am now reaching the age when a backward glance at the terrain I have traversed may be justified. Because this is a systematization and overview of my own work, the reader will find only an illustrative use of the literature in the many fields to which I refer. More detailed references are available in the three volumes mentioned above.

In the first and second chapters I shall be concerned with theoretical assumptions discussed only incidentally in my previous publications. The four chapters which follow present overviews of the three comparative studies I have mentioned, albeit with an emphasis on their theoretical implications.

Berkeley, California
September 1982

One

Rationalism and Historicism in the Social Sciences

I

Imagine a twenty-two-year-old German-Jewish refugee, coming to America in 1938 to start his studies at the University of Chicago. I had been initiated into the reading of serious books by my father, who helped me with the difficulties I encountered. Study, in those last years of the Weimar Republic and the early years of the Hitler regime, even without any academic preparation (and in considerable social isolation), had given me a kind of defense against the world surrounding me. This was my background for coping with the intellectual contentions that prevailed in the Department of Sociology at the University of Chicago.

One of the two main positions in the department was represented by Robert Park, who was a former student of Georg Simmel and who had earlier on been an investigative reporter. Here, across the Atlantic, Simmel's sociology had become under Park's leadership an empirical investigation of life histories, of occupations and ways of life, of ethnic or residential neighborhoods. Such titles as *The Schoolteacher, The Ghetto,* and *The Gold-Coast and the Slum* are representative of this literature. But by the time I arrived in 1938, these interests of the 1920s were already abating. A second position was becoming dominant, based on demography and the study of public opinion with a heavy emphasis on research methods. Spokesmen for both positions claimed to be scientific, but there was little agreement among them. To the first group, the study of attitudes was removed from experience and of little sociological interest. And to the second group, life histories and studies of subcultures were sociological impressionism lacking in methodological rigor. There were many qualifications on both sides, of course, but this contrast points to the heart of the matter.

These arguments influenced me. Research, I was persuaded, should follow a positivist program at least to some extent. One should have answers to such questions as: What do I want to know? What kind of evidence is suitable to prove a point? How can it be assembled? Are there good reasons for assuming that certain facts can either prove or disprove the original contention? One will not find answers if one does not specify what one wants to know. Although I felt receptive toward a positivist approach, my attitude could not help but be influenced as well by the contemporary political conditions of 1938–1941. My American teachers insisted on the strict separation between scholarship and partisanship. Their approach was bound to impress me because I had seen so much partisanship in the preceding years under the Nazis. To achieve dispassion and nonpartisanship meant a great deal to me, as did the demand for reliable proof. I had just come from a country in which racism had been broadcast with all the pretense of science but none of the substance.

Still, I was not entirely convinced by the positivist approach. There was no denying that answers are impossible so long as the questions are not clear, but one has to know a great deal before one can pose clear and interesting questions. Preliminary inquiries necessarily precede any question worth asking, as they do the formulation of a hypothesis. I resisted the idea that these inquiries are not a part of science. Yet the positivists among my teachers tended to restrict the realm of science to the logic of proof. By neglecting the logic of discovery because it was really not very logical and could not be taught easily, they seemed to support the view that unproved and, above all, unprovable assertions have no place in science. That did not make sense if a science without presuppositions is impossible. At the time, some people mocked that social scientists knew more and more about less and less—and this was not without some justification, in view of the emphasis on method at the expense of substance. It seemed to me that the "logic of discovery" had to be brought into some appropriate relation to the "logic of proof." In struggling with this question as a graduate student I became preoccupied with the ideal of science as a problem in its own right, and this preoccupation has remained with me since.

A paradox besets the social sciences. For two centuries, the belief in progress seemed to be associated with an increasing distrust of man. In his book *Wahrheit und Ideologie* (1945), the Swiss philosopher Hans Barth had shown that our advancing knowledge of man consisted in part in a greater understanding of human irrationality.[1] This insight suggested to me that by their emphasis on methodological rigor some social scientists hoped to counteract a growing skepticism, as if the belief in science could still the doubts concerning human rationality. Later, the "fetishism of science" became a fashionable slogan. But such concerns should not be addressed with slogans. The questions of the belief in science refer to pervasive social phenomena which have been rediscovered in our time, particularly in relation to the study of social change.

Until World War II, American social scientists gave most of their attention to problems of American society; they do so still. But since the end of the war many of them have become concerned with the "developing countries," recognizing that the stark poverty of these countries goes together with their political instability. What makes for self-sustained economic growth, what leads to political stability? The prevailing scholarly approach to these questions has been that further advances of knowledge are needed to facilitate the economic development and stabilize the political order of the so-called Third World.

One manifestation of this belief is the "scientific" background of American development aid, the first topic of the following discussion. The second topic is the recent development of a theoretical interest in comparative studies of change which applies accepted research procedures to these studies in the belief that problems of change should be approached like any other subject of investigation. I shall contrast this "rationalistic" approach with an "historicist" one, which differs from the rationalistic in its skepticism toward science in relation to studies of social change and by its lesser expectations concerning the benefits to be derived from knowledge. In the concluding part of this chapter, several theoretical approaches will be examined which subscribe to the "rationalistic" approach: the technocratic, the ahistorical with a psychological or a political emphasis, and the quasi-Marxist approach. These approaches overlap at many points. During the past twenty years all of them have influenced comparative social research in the United States, and all of them are concerned with "modernization." This description and assessment should be sufficient to provide the background for an analysis in Chapter 2 of the "historicist" perspective, which has guided my own studies.

II

At the end of World War II, Europe was devastated. We all know that from 1947 to 1951 the European economies were restored through a massive infusion of American capital. The experience of the Marshall Plan seemed to suggest that massive assistance would soon be followed by rapid changes throughout the affected economies. Once the effect of assistance had been felt in fact, the internal momentum and interdependence of each economy took over, so that the need for further outside assistance declined. Their recovery was under way, the European economies returned to the position of competitors among themselves and with the United States.

For a time, this Marshall Plan model of assistance reinforced the benign view that the self-sustained development of backward economies could also be achieved through programs of assistance and investment. In this perspective, technical assistance to underdeveloped countries appeared both humanitarian and useful; for, if properly administered, such assistance would speed the process of economic change. In the American setting, this whole undertaking was initiated with a great deal of goodwill, and some of today's technical aid programs (as well as the Peace Corps) retain this sense of a secular mission. But over the years the early enthusiasm has waned, funds have been curtailed, and awareness of difficulties in the field have mounted.

As Michael Todaro has written:

> The Marshall Plan for Europe worked because the European countries receiving aid possessed the necessary structural, institutional and attitudinal conditions (e.g., well-integrated commodity and money markets, highly developed transport facilities, well-trained and educated manpower, the motivation to succeed, an efficient government bureaucracy, etc.) to convert new capital effectively into higher levels of output . . . [In many cases] these same attitudes and arrangements are not present in underdeveloped nations nor are the complementary factors such as managerial competence, skilled labor and the ability to plan and administer a wide assortment of development projects always present in sufficient quantities.[2]

After a generation of effort, the conclusion seems unavoidable that aid programs to countries of the Third World cannot compare in their effect with the impact of the Marshall Plan on the economies of western Europe—even if one takes account of the great differences between the two kinds of aid programs. The poorer countries of the world cannot quickly develop the attitudes and institutions required for economic development, as Todaro's statement suggests.

Very uneasy feelings recur as one thinks of the vast contrast between rich and poor countries, and it seems at times that writings on economic development seek to quiet these feelings through models based on the belief in science. Such models often depend on evolutionary assumptions and organic analogies with a long history in Western thought. Evolutionism seems best suited to cope intellectually with the stark contrast between the industrialized nations of the world and all those other countries which euphemisms call developing or less developed in order not to call them destitute and backward. It is more comfortable to acknowledge the contrast between rich and poor nations if one can assume that the latter are indeed on their way toward self-sustained economic growth. And this result seems assured if it is assumed that sooner or later every society passes through similar stages of development.[3]

Meanwhile, assistance can be offered to help these countries help themselves, and in this context an ancillary set of assumptions has proved serviceable. Societies are conceived as systems which possess a high degree of interdependence. Changes in one part are inevitably followed by changes in other parts. This interdependence is regulated internally: particular variables may change only within specifiable limits. As a corollary, systems are marked off by boundaries, with the inside clearly separated from the outside. If on these assumptions we develop a knowledge of what goes with what, then an intervention based on such knowledge (like technical assistance) should, or would, or could enable a country to develop its economic and political institutions.

This intellectual approach to the "modernization" problem is usually supported by a before-and-after model of the society under investigation. The earlier and the later social structure are distinguished via two groups of dichotomous attributes. It then becomes difficult to resist the view that each group of attributes constitutes a generalizable system of interrelated variables, like "tradition" and "modernity." On that assumption, societies can be classified in terms of their relative approximation of one or the other cluster of attributes. And this procedure leads to a rank order of countries based on their relative degree of modernization.

III

Social scientists have always been interested in social change, and this interest has increased since World War II. Comparison is not new as an analytic method. Guy Swanson has stated that "thinking without comparison is unthinkable.[4] Even our vocabulary of general terms like social class or society has meaning only through the implicit comparison of these terms with status group or community. Thus comparison becomes almost synonymous with rational or scientific. But there is also a non-trivial sense of comparative analysis of social change, often called historical sociology, which should be distinguished from causal analyses in sociology, methodologically as well as substantively. I turn to this distinction between trivial and non-trivial comparisons in order to explicate the theoretical assumptions of historical sociology, and of my own studies as well.

One gets at this non-trivial sense most easily by starting with the general attributes of scientific inquiry. As Neil Smelser has stated:

> The process of gaining empirical control over sources of variation is clarified by referring to the distinction between causal conditions treated as *parameters* and causal conditions treated as *operative variables*. Parameters are conditions that are known or suspected to influence a dependent variable but, in the investigation at hand, are assumed or made not to vary. Operative variables are conditions that are known or suspected to influence the dependent variable and, in the investigation, are allowed or made to vary in order to assess this influence. By converting variables into parameters, most of the potentially operative conditions are made not to vary, so that the influence of one or a few conditions may be isolated and analyzed. . . . All methods of scientific inquiry, and those striving to approximate it, rest on the systematic manipulation and control of parameters and variables.[5]

Scholars like Swanson and Smelser see no reason to treat historical materials differently from any others. Data of every kind demand the methods of inquiry most appropriate to them. For the rest, we must transform, by further manipulation, some aspect of the parameters of what we have put under the "all other things being equal" clause into operational variables that can be studied. But this assumption ignores that social scientists, as well as their sociopolitical data, are a part of the historical process. To suggest further manipulation of parameters and variables always implies a commitment to the Baconian view that "human knowledge and human power meet in one; for where the cause is not known, the effect cannot be produced. Nature to be commanded must be obeyed."[6] Bacon's dicta push us in the direction of assuming that once we obey nature, we can then command it. In this way we approach our studies in the expectation that knowledge is a token of human power.

We should consider two questions regarding the scientific procedure described by Smelser. First, is it the case that students of society can "manipulate and control" their data in roughly the same manner as do natural scientists? Second, can we set aside without further ado that students of society and history are themselves a part of the society and history they study? My answer to both questions is no. Social scientists are severely restricted in the manipulation of their data, and their involvement in society and history is a part of their study as the natural scientist's place in history is not.[7] The rising American interest in comparative studies since World War II is itself an example of that involvement in social change which is not an object of experimental or hypothetical manipulation.

It follows that scholars and their objects of study, subject and object, are a part of society and history. This is the context in which the social scientist commits himself to do research. I want to characterize that commitment specifically in terms of the purpose for which knowledge is pursued. To this end I distinguish between two styles of scholarship,[8] well knowing that the distinction is rather artificial (like all such types) and that the two labels I employ, rationalistic and historicist, are easily misused.*

The *rationalistic* search for truth seeks to develop methods which will ultimately make the right understanding compelling to all who seek truth. In this view, understanding is the work of reason emancipated from all forms of unreason like emotions and partisanship. A prominent feature of this approach is its inattention to the historical setting of the search for truth. At the beginning of modern science, Francis Bacon exemplified this approach

---

*The two terms employed are idiosyncratic because I want them understood only in the way I have defined them. Rationalism and rationalist have an accepted meaning in the history of ideas, as historicism does not; the first term is descriptive, the second polemical. But I want to use both terms in this polemical or invidious fashion, hence the terms rationalistic and historicist. I cannot use rational and historical, which would be simpler, because there are rational positions which are not as committed to the idea of progress as the rationalistic position is. And there are historical approaches which are not as self-conscious about the mutability of scholarly inquiry as the historicist position is. Further, the rationalistic position does not exclude historical materials, nor is the historicist position anti-rationalist. These complexities help account for the fact that Karl Popper's attack in *The Poverty of Historicism* (1961) is aimed at the rationalistic position, as I describe it, but not at rationalism nor at historicism. In a late preface (1959) Professor Popper admitted as much when he explained that his rather puzzling title was "intended as an allusion to the title of Marx's book *The Poverty of Philosophy.*"

not only by his typology of idols, the errors of reasoning into which men fall time and again. He also revealed the historical setting of science, when he defended it against the charge of heresy and at the same time invited the support of science by men of affairs, who had power and resources but lacked understanding. In this approach truth is achieved, once the proper methods of inquiry are applied. If the quest for knowledge does not succeed, then either the wrong questions were asked or the wrong methods were used, or both. Underlying this approach is the belief in progress through the cumulation of knowledge.

The *historicist* search for truth asserts that for all who seek truth the right understanding can be made compelling only for a time—even with the best available methods. Historical conditions change, and that means the facts and their contexts, as well as the scholars with their interests and methods. The old Latin proverb applies: *tempora mutantur et nos mutamur in illis.* In the historicist approach, understanding is also the work of reason emancipated from emotion, partisanship, and other idols of the mind. Truth is achieved once the proper methods are applied; this is not a matter of results being invalidated by the fact that they (like all results) depend on a ceteris paribus assumption that many parameters must be ignored if selected variables are to be studied systematically. Nevertheless, understanding remains conditional, because the scholar and society, subject and object, are aspects of history and undergo change. Hence the truths that are discovered tend to be of limited interest and applicability, and they will be replaced by other truths that are likely to be equally limited. Underlying this approach is the belief that man's interest in truth changes, and hence that knowledge of society is not cumulative, or that it is cumulative only to a limited extent.[9]

These two positions have many variants which diminish the contrast, but I think a bold statement should be made about the main difference between them. Both approaches to knowledge have here been defined in terms of their respective purposes, emphasizing the hopes or expectations of the scholar. Another definition might distinguish the two approaches in methodological terms, contrasting the analysis of variables from that of structural contexts. Here one can speak of indeterminacy because one can analyze variables *or* contexts, but hardly both of them simultaneously.

Our ideas concerning the purpose of knowledge have consequences. A belief in progress through the cumulation of knowledge differs from the belief that knowledge is worthwhile even if there is little cumulation and the future is uncertain. Still, the search for truth, whether in its rationalistic or its historicist mode, presupposes a belief in the value of truth, and such a belief implies an answer to the question, "Value for what?"

Wherever the cumulation of knowledge is identified with progress, the indifferent or negative side effects of increased knowledge are discounted. There are many arguments to support this position. We never know what cannot be known. We cannot foretell the good and bad side effects of new knowledge. And failure to seek new knowledge implies a preference for ignorance. Progress through knowledge means putting the values of new knowledge above the risk of negative side effects, probably on the assumption that the future is always at risk and that increased knowledge will enhance our ability to cope with negative results.

The historicist search for truth is in a different position because it is not sustained by a belief in progress. The evidence for the cumulation of knowledge outside the natural sciences is modest at best. In the social sciences, methods of validation are often inconclusive, and our interest in what is worth knowing changes in response to historical circumstances. Advances in relation to previously verified knowledge are often inconclusive.

In addition, we are of many minds concerning our desire to know the future. In his reflections on world history, Jacob Burckhardt observed that all human desire and endeavor would be utterly confused if a man knew beforehand the exact time of his death, or a people the century of their downfall. Burckhardt still believed, as do I, that the quest for knowledge is worthwhile. There are always new things still to be discovered; and we have more knowledge of past and present societies than any previous age has had. This can be a sign of cultural enrichment and a basis for understanding among men, even if it is not considered a token of progress through knowledge. On the other hand, Burckhardt did not think knowledge of the future feasible. A future known in advance would foreclose the appearance of anything new; it is literally a contradiction in terms. Nor did he believe such prediction desirable, because men act in the present with hopes and fears that are undiminished by knowledge of the outcome.[10]

The contrast between the rationalistic and the historicist positions is great. But the two have one common element which is important for an understanding of comparative historical sociology. No inquiry can be undertaken without at least an implicit commitment to a purpose. A clear avowal of purpose is especially important in the social sciences, where that purpose is often debatable. For in the absence of stating our purpose of inquiry, we run the danger of mistaking different results or judgments for what are in fact different inquiries. When we initiate these inquiries, our purpose in doing so involves the future. Our purposes always involve hopes and fears concerning the possible uses and misuses of the knowledge we seek. Ultimately, these hopes and fears reflect our image of man and society, our beliefs about what men are capable of doing. Inquiry in the social sciences thus involves our judgment about man's future based on an implicit assessment of his past and present.

For these reasons, the consequences should be explored which follow from the rationalistic and the historicist positions. In the rationalistic search for truth, the goal of cumulative knowledge and hence the belief in progress are (or until recently were considered to be) a sufficient moral justification. In the remainder of this chapter, several studies of modernization will be examined in order to explicate the rationalistic purposes of knowledge their authors have had in mind. The first of these studies exemplifies a technocratic theory of society.

IV

The great merit of Daniel Lerner's study *The Passing of Traditional Society* is its candid use of Western modernization as a model of global applicability. For Marx, England, as the country that is "most developed industrially," exemplified universal "laws of capitalist development"; for Lerner, Western modernization exhibits "certain components and sequences whose relevance is global."[11] He recognizes that the "North Atlantic area" developed first and rather gradually, whereas other countries came later and sought to develop more rapidly; but, like Marx, he dismisses this as a secondary consideration. As Lerner sees it, the central proposition is that in the process of modernization, then as now, four sectors or dimensions are related systematically to one another: urbanization, literacy, media participation, and political participation.[12] Lerner believes that the high association between these four factors points to an underlying systemic coherence, which he calls the "participant style of life." But at the same time he asserts that "traditional societies exhibit extremely variant growth patterns; some are more urban than literate, others more media participant than urban." Such "deviations from the regression line" are due to the fact that "people don't do what, on any rational course of behavior, they should do"— hardly a consistent behaviorist statement, which should have prompted him to reconsider the assumptions of his scientific model.

Lerner's model fails to do justice to the reality of the backward countries. I quote David Riesman, who has written an introductory commentary to the new edition of the book:

> The general belief that there must be a way—a way out of poverty and the psychic constriction of the "Traditionals"—links the author of this volume with his own national tradition. But this very American belief that there is a way is a dream. And Professor Lerner, as a student of communications, understands that it is dreams that inspire not only new wants but new solutions—as well as violent gestures towards modernity. What seems required from his perspective is an allopathic rationing of dreams, enough to spark the religion of progress, of advance, without inciting to riot.[13]

Riesman adds (after all, he also is an American) that the "emotional and political fluency of newly-liberated illiterates can be quite terrifying."

These remarks are not meant to dismiss with easy irony either the idea of evolution or the preoccupation with the tragic contrast between rich and poor countries. The burning question remains how this contrast can be overcome. But the intellectual tools with which American social scientists have approached these problems are not adequate to the task, though I must add that I cannot offer a solution either. I shall confine myself rather to considerations which go beyond the evolutionary model, but which also remain bound up with the belief in science. Still, though I cannot claim to solve the problem as a whole, I think I can lead away from a *one*-sided rationalism and toward a comparative historical approach to the issues involved.

It was recognized at an early time that the industrialization of Western European countries represented a questionable model for a comparative study of modernization, and yet it is in fact difficult to be free of this historical precedent. After all, one can hardly avoid thinking of these Western countries when one thinks of an industrial society, particularly because "latecomers" like Japan and Russia have used them as models for their own development. It seemed promising, therefore, when in *Industrialism and Industrial Man* Clark Kerr and his collaborators constructed a "logic of industrialism," an abstraction which starts from the assumption that all countries in transition will eventuate in a completely industrialized society.

The authors emphasize that the industrializing tendencies they have deducted (albeit by illustrative reference to the experience of "developed" societies) are not likely to be fully realized in the actual course of history. Yet, throughout the volume phrases recur which betray a confusion between these two levels of analysis. On the same page tendencies are alternately called logically constructed and inherent.[14] Emphasis on the contrast between abstraction and history is followed by the assertion that "the empire of industrialism will embrace the whole world." Industrialization is called an "invincible process," and the uncertainties of the future are relegated to variations of length and difficulty in the transition, or to the several types of past industrializations.[15] Perhaps the most arresting feature of this deterministic view of the future is that the industrialism of the whole world is predicated, not on the organization of production, as in Marx, but on the initiating or manipulating actions of five different elites whose capacity to industrialize whole societies is simply assumed. Exceptions and delays are seen as deviations which "cannot prevent the transformation in the long run."[16] Neither the possibility of failure nor the possibility of unprecedented types of industrialization is given serious consideration. Seldom has social change been interpreted in so managerial a fashion, whereas all contingencies of action are treated as mere historical variations which cannot alter the "logic of industrialism." Though the recognition of alternate routes to industrialization is a distinct improvement over the unilinear evolutionism of Lerner's study, the authors abandon their gain when they predict one system of industrialism for all societies in much the same way as Marx predicted the end of class struggles and of prehistory for the socialist society of the future. But in this case a typology of industrializing elites is substituted for Marx's theory of the class struggle.

V

Two important attempts have been made to cope intellectually with the problem of modernization in ahistorical terms. Again, I am concerned with types of explanation, not with the details of particular research projects. One study deals with the psychological preconditions and corollaries of modernization. The other approach is concerned with the political institutions and behavior patterns suggested by the phrase "the civic culture." The social-psychological approach is deliberately ahistorical. The political one has the same ahistorical tendency, but over the years some uncertainty has crept into it with the result that these studies now vacillate between rationalistic and historicist tendencies, probably without intending to do so. In both studies one finds traces of the faith in science.

In the social-psychological approach, one encounters quickly the familiar contrast between tradition and modernity which goes back to the distinction between *Gemeinschaft* and *Gesellschaft* as introduced by Ferdinand Toennies. It is quite plausible that particular patterns of behavior and attitude correlate with a certain type of society. By applying the methods of modern public opinion research, one can conduct comparative sample studies in different countries in order to examine these correlations and to answer the question how closely the personality types ascertained by the research approximate the type best adapted to a modern industrial society. Alex Inkeles and David Smith have conducted such an investigation, and they state their intellectual agenda at the outset. They want to

1. make the common man, not the elite, the focus of their research, in order to do justice to the personal as against the institutional aspect of economic development;
2. counteract the overemphasis on the first six years of life which is characteristic of many studies of personality;
3. develop a more precise understanding of the impact of living conditions upon adults; to do this they attribute decisive importance to the factory (the organization of work) independently of political and cultural conditions.

Finally, they hope to show in their study, *Becoming Modern,* that modernization is not associated regularly with high psychic costs.[17]

Interesting as this study is, it leads to the question whether the facts excluded by its purposes and methods can indeed be regarded as insignificant for the process of modernization. If one excludes the influence of elites, the cultural and political contexts of economic development, then certainly one cannot assess their historical significance—quite aside from the question whether the factory exerts the same influence on "personal modernization."

The political approach to modernization was initiated with the volume *The Politics of the Developing Areas,* published in 1960. In the intervening years, eight further volumes of this series have followed. Gabriel Almond, who initiated the series, contributed an introduction to the first volume in which he gave special attention to the conceptual problems of comparative studies. He was concerned with the applicability of the usual social science concepts to the developing areas because those concepts had been formulated in the context of Western European history, and their applicability had become questionable as one moved away from the European contexts. Almond concluded that the familiar concepts should be abandoned altogether. The purpose of this exercise does not consist only in a thoroughgoing avoidance of ethnocentrism. Even more important is the attempt to develop a single conceptual framework for all generically similar political phenomena. Both purposes make good sense from the standpoint of a theory of science, however difficult their implementation may be in fact.

The spirit of this undertaking is manifested in the following quotation:

> The search for new concepts . . . reflects an underlying drift towards a new and coherent way of thinking about and studying politics that is implied in such slogans as the "behavioral approach." This urge towards a new conceptual unity is suggested when we compare the new terms with the old. Thus, instead of the concept of the "state," limited as it is by legal and institutional meanings, we prefer "political system"; instead of "powers," which again is a legal concept in connotation, we are beginning to prefer "functions"; instead of "offices" (legal again), we prefer "roles"; instead of "institutions," which again directs us toward formal norms, "structures"; instead of "public opinion" and "citizenship training," formal and rational in meaning, we prefer "political culture" and "political socialization." We are not setting aside public law and philosophy as disciplines, but simply telling them to move over to make room for a growth in political theory that has been long overdue.[18]

The intention is evident to conceive of politics as a universal phenomenon, a perfectly sensible objective in the context of a scientific system-theory. But this procedure means at the same time that the distinction between societies with or without a state (or monopoly of legitimate force) is lost sight of, or abandoned altogether. And this is proposed just at the time when the developing areas are preoccupied with state formation and with the construction of viable governments because success in these efforts appears to promise considerable gains in public welfare.

Accordingly, Almond and his collaborators have made evident their considerable ambivalence between rationalism and historicism. As acute analysts of international politics, they know only too well that politicians of the Third World do not have much truck with the abstractions of science. To the people concerned it makes little difference whether and how politics can be analyzed by generally applicable concepts. They are preoccupied with their own interests and the development of their country, and they know well enough how to distinguish between a government that works and one that idles or has destructive consequences. Therefore, they also know that a legal system can be an important ingredient of a government that works. Their problem is how to combine such a system with their culture and institutions, including the quasi-legal ones, but this problem the social sciences tend to "address" with their universal conceptual language. Political scientists in particular speak of states, powers, offices, institutions, public opinion, and education in citizenship—all phenomena from whose internal logic Almond's universally applicable concepts were to set us free.

Thus, we return once more to the peculiarity of Western societies, and we do so in good company. For in their volume *The Civic Culture* (1963), Almond and Sidney Verba have investigated empirically a number of Western societies with special reference to their different variants of that noted peculiarity. In this connection, they recognize obviously that differences such as that between England and Germany have historic foundations which have important repercussions down to the present. Not only that: the series of volumes which began with the program of a universal conceptual language in 1960 has arrived meanwhile at the historical development of national states. The seventh and eighth volumes provide little reading matter concerned with the original program of universal concepts for political science.

The reason for this change of emphasis is easy to understand, since all social scientists interested in comparative studies find themselves in the same dilemma. In grappling with historical materials we cannot do without concepts—like all historians, by the way. But the proper reach of these concepts is a perennial concern. Concepts lose their capacity to tell us much of anything if their scope is too broad, but they cannot transcend the individual case if their scope is too narrow. I believe we need typological groupings of societies, however difficult it is to work with such groupings. We need a characterization of what is distinctive about European compared with East Asian or Latin American development. Experience shows that most scholars group themselves in this regional fashion because they find common problems in the countries with which they are concerned, as well as propositions which apply to more than one country of the region. Why not utilize the sense developed by scholars of a region that the countries of which they are composed have a certain family likeness?

VI

In this survey of treatises on modernization, attention should also be given to Marxism, which became popular at American universities only after World War II. Marx emphasized the scientific character of his analysis of capitalism. One need only think of the confidence with which he took physics for the model of his approach—that he wrote of the "natural law of capitalist development" and of tendencies that would lead "with iron necessity to inevitable results." In these terms, his approach certainly appears rationalistic. But Marx also made the historical conditioning of knowledge and truth a central point of his analysis, and in this respect he is indebted to an historicist perspective. Moreover, he made the future of all mankind the purpose of his investigations. To this day the powerful attraction of Marxism consists in this combination of scientific claims, historicism, a radical critique of the status quo, and the confidence that this analysis of capitalism is itself a step toward an ideal future.

The Marxist belief in science can be contrasted with the scientific skepticism of the historicist approach. Historicism does not deny that knowledge can mean power, but many of its spokesmen add that knowledge reveals human impotence as well. The belief in progress through science has become questionable, as, for example, in the work of the French historian Fernand Braudel, whose work has had increasing influence on historical sociology in America during recent years. That is why I mention him here, though his work actually has only an indirect relation to this context because it lacks faith in science and has little to do with Marxism. Yet Braudel is relevant all the same because he is an extreme reductionist, and thus has a strong affinity with one prevailing tendency in modern social science, and also because he has given a decisive impetus to modern American Marxism, probably without intending to do so. In his great work *The Mediterranean and the Mediterranean World in the Age of Philip II,* Braudel distinguishes the structures of geologic and geographic history from the conjunctures of social history (like demographic and economic trends). Both of these are often submerged, slow-moving and discernible only in retrospect. Both differ in this respect from the manifest historical events and individual actors which only appear to be significant but in fact are not. Here is Braudel's final, philosophical reflection:

> So when I think of the individual, I am always inclined to see him imprisoned within a destiny in which he himself has little hand, fixed in a landscape in which the infinite perspectives of the long term stretch into the distance both behind him and before. In historical analysis as I see it, rightly or wrongly, the long run always wins in the end. Annihilating innumerable events—all those which cannot be accommodated in the main ongoing current and which are therefore ruthlessly swept to one side—it indubitably limits both the freedom of the individual and even the role of chance. I am by temperament a "structuralist," little tempted by the event, or even by the short-term conjuncture which is after all merely a grouping of events in the same area.[19]

This resigned conclusion should be read with some awareness of Braudel's afterthoughts. He emphasized that his work was planned in collaboration with Lucien Febvre, whose projected "Western Thought and Belief, 1400–1880" was to have been the companion piece to Braudel's volume. The Febvre book did not appear, and Braudel believes that his own later work on capitalism cannot be understood without analyzing politics, culture, and social structure.[20] Still, I doubt that Febvre's work or such further studies would have altered Braudel's emphasis on the long run.

For some five years during World War II, Braudel was a prisoner of war in Mainz, Germany, where he wrote the major part of his book on the Mediterranean. He felt that his tendency to view history in terms of slow change over the long term was greatly reinforced by the personal isolation of captivity, and by the feeling that his deprivations of the moment were nothing in comparison with the slow, majestic change of natural forces.[21] His structuralist emphasis was strongly reinforced by captivity; it was not caused by it, for the book had been researched earlier. The book's mood was influenced by the trauma of France's defeat in two world wars and by the agonies of French decolonization. Presumably, there was some consolation in seeing these cataclysmic events as surface perturbations which did not greatly affect long-term changes in climate or long-term fluctuations of economic development. Important aspects of the human condition come into view when history is approached in this contemplative manner.

But what happens to the rationale of this position once it is transferred to the United States? The contemplative attitude which Braudel exemplifies was lost, even as his determinism, his emphasis on the long term of capitalist development, and his analysis of world economic dependencies were adopted. Braudel's ideas have been taken over by people associated with a world political orientation based on a Marxism of American design.

There are at least three reasons for the rising popularity of Marxism during the last decades, especially among historical sociologists in America, although almost everyone criticizes Marxism in many particulars or as a whole. First, Marx anticipated almost every critique of capitalism which has been voiced since his time, so that analyses of modern culture sound somehow Marxist even though they may have nothing to do with Marxism. Second, Marx's approach rested on a philosophical theory of man and society which combined the analysis of past and present societies with an anticipation of the future. This combination of science with prophecy exerts a powerful attraction, even if important parts of the theory are no longer convincing. Third, Marxism is characterized by its explanation of exploitation and power and is distinguished thereby from the approaches to modernization mentioned earlier. The Marxist explanation of national and international exploitation may have unsolved problems of its own, but it does deal with the glaring contrasts between riches and poverty. Consequently, one need not be committed to Marxism as a whole but can still be at liberty to use one or another of its propositions as a guideline for research.

This freewheeling use of Marxism can be illustrated by examining Immanuel Wallerstein's work, which combines elements of rationalism and historicism—a belief in science with prophecy, though hardly in Marx's philosophical manner. Wallerstein is a declared disciple of Braudel and the founder of the Fernand Braudel Center for the Study of Economics, Historical Systems, and Civilizations at the State University of New York in Binghamton. A trained sociologist, he originally specialized in African studies. In the 1970s Wallerstein turned to the comparative study of economic history, and he has become known as the author of a two-volume work, *The Modern World System* (1974, 1980), and of a volume of essays, *The Capitalist World Economy* (1979). In these writings, Wallerstein advances a radical position according to which the distinction between history and social science is outdated and the distinction between politics and scholarship fictitious.[22] Braudel looks upon the long term as a vantage point from which to contemplate the human condition with some detachment, a matter of temperament, as he says. By contrast, Wallerstein uses the same vantage point as a scholar and activist who believes that his analysis can undo the inequalities of this world—in the long run. "The long run always wins in the end": men have no role to play in history, at least none that really matters. Braudel comes to this conclusion with resignation, but for Wallerstein this thought is an expression of hope, even confidence.

His starting point is a radical critique of the conventional units of analysis like society, state, nation, or people—quite unlike Braudel's acceptance of a conventional geographic and cultural unit like the Mediterranean. Wallerstein has no difficulty in showing that all these terms, like any term taken from ordinary language, have overlapping meanings and are difficult to define unambiguously. His alternative is a threefold division of world history into mini-systems based on a "reciprocal lineage" mode of production (like tribes or other small-scale societies), world empires based on a "redistributive-tributary" mode (like the Chinese or Roman empires), and the world economy based on the capitalist mode. For the sake of simplicity, and in line with the author's own emphasis, I confine my remarks to this third type, which has existed since the sixteenth century.[23]

Wallerstein contends that states (to use only one of his examples) are not in fact total systems, and that—leaving small societies aside—only world systems are "real" social systems.[24]

> A world-system is a social system, one that has boundaries, struc-
> tures, member groups, rules of legitimation, and coherence. Its life
> is made up of the conflicting forces which hold it together by
> tension, and tear it apart as each group seeks eternally to remold it
> to its advantage. . . . It has a life-span over which its characteris-
> tics change in some respects and remain stable in others. . . .
> What characterizes a social system in my view is the fact that life
> within it is largely self-contained, and that the dynamics of its
> development are largely internal.[25]

Two pages later he tells us that the size of the world economy
depends upon the state of technology, especially transport and
communication, which are constantly changing phenomena.
Hence, the boundaries of the world economy are "ever fluid,"
and, one might add, so are the other attributes mentioned: structures, member groups, rules of legitimation, and coherence.

If this is so, then why is the world economy a "real" social
system, whereas the state is not? After all, states also possess
boundaries, structures, member groups, rules of legitimation, and
coherence, and over the centuries these attributes are "ever
fluid" as well. The answer cannot be in the long term because
Wallerstein's world economy has existed since the sixteenth century, whereas states like England or China, with their changing
boundaries and structures, have existed for much longer periods.
Nevertheless, the author decided that neither sovereign states nor
national societies are social systems; only the world economy is.
On this assumption, "changes in the sovereign states" can be
explained "as consequent upon the evolution and interaction of
the world-system." The apparently distinguishable societies of
the world can all be interpreted as operative variables of the
world economy just as the astronomer interprets different constellations as parts of one universe. The history of the modern
world economy is synonymous with the history of capitalism; and
capitalism "has been able to flourish because the world-economy
has had within its bounds . . . a multiplicity of political systems."
Because, according to Wallerstein, one can "only speak of social
change in social systems," and the world-economy is the only
social system of the modern world, it follows that this is the only
viable level of abstraction for the study of social change.[26]

Or is it? Why use world economy and world system and capi-

talism when the three terms are synonyms? Why speak of the
world economy as the only "*real*" social system, when the whole
context and the terms employed refer to abstractions that are
more or less useful? Wallerstein is candid enough to state that for
him (and, he thinks, for everyone else) scholarship and politics
are indistinguishable.[27] He believes in the eventual inevitability of
a socialist world government, not as a present possibility or in the
near future, but in the long run. At one point he speaks of a
socialist world government only as a third possible form of world
system (in addition to world empires like ancient Rome, or the
world economy of capitalism).[28] But at another point he writes of
the socialist mode of production as "our future world government. We are living in the transition to it, which will continue for
some time to come."[29] This is at least as "concrete" as Marx's
image of a socialist society without a division of labor. Given this
goal which is sure to come, Wallerstein is free to concentrate on
the mode of production as the sole determinant of history—in the
famous long run.

Here the difficulties are greater. The author does not have
Braudel's contemplative approach and temperament, which allows some room for alternative perspectives; nor does he rest his
case on philosophical considerations, as Marx did in his early
writings. Instead we are presented with the statement that "any
complex of ideas can be manipulated to serve any particular social or political objective."[30] As a result of this assumption, the
leap into the future becomes easy. Wallerstein observes the conflicts of nation-states in a capitalist world economy, but he desires
and predicts the emergence of a socialist world government. How
does he move from his observation to his goal? Thus:

> Since states are the primary arena of political conflict in a capital-
> ist world-economy, and since the functioning of the world-econ-
> omy is such that national class composition varies widely, it is easy
> to perceive why the politics of states differentially located in rela-
> tion to the world-economy should be so dissimilar. It is also then
> easy to perceive that using the political machinery of a given state
> to change the social composition and world-economic function of
> national production does not per se change the capitalist world-
> system as such.

> Obviously, however, these various national thrusts to a change

in structural position (which we misleadingly often call "development") do in fact affect, indeed over the long run do in fact transform, the world-system. But they do so via the intervening variable of their impact on world-wide class consciousness of the proletariat.[31]

National class struggles affect the position of a country in the world economy, and that position is bound to change; so in the long run a class-conscious world proletariat will result. This conclusion suggests that the shadow of a simplified Marxism has eclipsed the influence of Braudel. Wallerstein seems to have transposed Marx's analysis of a national class struggle onto an international canvas so that the rich countries of the world, whether they are capitalist or communist, now play the role of a world bourgeoisie, whereas the poor countries play the role of a world proletariat. The author says little about the road that might lead to a socialist world government—quite in contrast to Marx, who had a great deal to say about the road but very little about the future.

In reviewing Wallerstein's theoretical position, I have not attempted to do justice to his analyses of economic history from the emergence of capitalist agriculture in the sixteenth century to the mercantilist consolidation of the European world economy up to 1750. One reason is that two further volumes on nineteenth-century capitalism and the emerging tendencies toward the world proletarization of the poor countries and a socialist world government are still to come. The more important reason, however, is that from an historicist standpoint the questions asked must be examined first. Clearly, Wallerstein is not content with the contemplative temperament of his adoptive teacher Braudel or with the modest aspirations of an historicist position. He prefers Marx's belief in the eighteenth-century idea of progress through knowledge, though at the same time he discards Marx's tenet that "men make their own history." It was this tenet which made Marx an heir of the Baconian tradition who set out to *prove* that his analysis of capitalism would contribute to the revolutionary overthrow he was predicting. Perhaps Wallerstein's further volumes will show us how he can assume that "circumstances make human history" and still expect that his own analysis will contribute to a coming socialist world government—a government which, however, is to result entirely from the impersonal forces of the capitalist world economy.

One might almost think that Wallerstein had bridged the gap between a rationalistic and a historicist approach. On the one hand he uses the concept "system," and on the other he denies the distinction between science and politics, thus seeming to stand in both camps. But the idea of one capitalist world economy since the sixteenth century is unconvincing, both as the concept of one system and as the description of one and the same capitalism over that period of time. Nor is the unity of theory and practice of much weight, because it is without philosophical underpinning and appears to be without definite scientific or political implications. But Wallerstein's work has become quite influential despite its lack of theoretical refinement, presumably because his combination of theory and economic history appears to prove that the economic and political dependence of the Third World can be traced back to the sixteenth century. From his work it seems to follow that the capitalist world economy is the decisive cause of the economic backwardness of the Third World, that the world's riches are the cause of the world's poverty. This opinion plays a certain role today both in the internal politics of the West and in the international politics and the self-image of the Third World. Wallerstein participates quite deliberately in the ideological controversies of modern world politics, for the contrast between rich and poor countries is inseparable from these controversies.

But how are the controversies to be interpreted? Is this contrast between the developed and the underdeveloped world primarily due to that concatenation of circumstances which brought about a breakthrough to economic growth in the West during the sixteenth century, a concatenation which then had no parallel anywhere else? This is the internal explanation of capitalism. Or is the contrast primarily the result of Western dominance, which began in the late fifteenth century and gradually imposed economic and political dependency upon one country after another? This is the external, imperialist explanation of capitalism. This bitter debate is ideological and pointless, as Fernand Braudel has pointed out.

No one can exploit the world simply because he wants to do so.
He first must develop his power and consolidate it slowly. But it is
certain that, although this power is developed through a slow,
internal process, it is strengthened by the exploitation of other
parts of the world, and that, in the course of this double process,
the chasm separating the exploiter from the exploited constantly
deepens.[32]

Still, this valid argument will not make the ideological dispute
disappear. For the emphasis on the early breakthrough reminds
the poor countries of their own failure, whereas the emphasis on
imperialism and dependency reminds the rich countries of their
history of conquest and exploitation.

Two

Objective and Subjective Meaning in History

The rationalistic position continues to have a decisive influence today. True, the modern theory of science has raised questions concerning even the rationalist self-image of the natural sciences; but so far these questions have not diminished the dominance of rationalism.

By comparison, the historicist position is less well known, and the following discussion is addressed explicitly to an interpretation of this perspective. Once we accept that knowledge in the social sciences has been cumulative only to a very limited extent, we are more likely to take a stronger interest in what has previously been excluded: a fuller understanding—admittedly incomplete and partly intuitive—of the parameters of the search for knowledge and its objects of inquiry. Such understanding is especially called for when comparative historical studies are used in exploratory fashion to clarify the meaning of questions to be asked and the conditions under which answers to them are attempted. Such exploratory inquiries are not, or need not be, at odds with the search for the best methods of inquiry and hence the quest for valid knowledge. After all, if a question is worth asking, it is worth answering correctly. But now a great deal more depends upon the kind of questions we ask; our decisions on what to investigate are ultimately moral. Notice how the ground has shifted.

The historicist position does not abandon the search for truth. But as doubts rise concerning the cumulation of knowledge, the belief in progress necessarily weakens. Hence we must seek the moral justification of our (historicist) search for knowledge in the quality of the questions we ask as much as in the conscientious way we answer them. In this perspective, the parameters of scholarly inquiry, the "all other things being equal" clause, or simply the assumptions or presuppositions which precede every inquiry—these become objects of study in their own right. In pursuing this general theme, I am particularly concerned with the theoretical foundations of my own comparative studies.

My exposition proceeds in four steps. First, I wish to show that the historicist position arises from the subjective interests in our quest for knowledge and the mutability of cultural problems. Second, I shall describe some phases of the Western history of ideas which are marked by objectivist views of the world. Third, I shall show how and why Max Weber opposed this objectivist interpretation of history. The discussion concludes with a sketch of the contexts in which Weber's approach became significant for my work.

I

Social research is characterized by an interplay between identification and detachment, of subjectivity and objectivity. The social scientist must think social knowledge worthwhile. He must cultivate his interest in man and society, but also his detachment from them, for his observations should be as objective as possible. This combination of attitudes requires a congenial setting like that of the university. For social scientists depend upon institutional protection and organizational support, which presuppose the goodwill of the public as expressed in legal privileges, financial assistance, and other aids. We come full circle: to study society we require support, yet we regard the society supporting us with scholarly detachment. We are a part of the society from which we are detached by our research. As social scientists we cannot extricate ourselves from this first circle of social research.

The circle is reminiscent of the paradox of Zeno according to which a Cretan complains that all Cretans are liars. This paradox leads to an infinite series of mutually exclusive inferences, because the proposition asserts the general untruthfulness of the Cretans, but that untruthfulness confirms the truth of the proposition. If all Cretans are liars, then the Cretan making that statement is also a liar; then it is a lie that all Cretans are liars, and he may be telling the truth. But if it is true that they all lie, then this Cretan may lie too; then some Cretans (including this one) may tell the truth, and so on. Modern logic teaches, if I understand it correctly, that Zeno's paradox is no paradox at all, but rather a logically impermissible inference. For the proposition that all Cretans are liars, a factual assertion, is here brought into question by the circumstance that the person making the assertion is a Cretan. Because he belongs to the world of those to whom the statement refers, doubts arise concerning the validity of what he has said. But logic tells us that these doubts depend upon a false inference, because statements about matters of fact must be distinguished clearly from statements about persons who make statements; the object must be distinguished from the subject. The proposition that all Cretans are liars may be true or false without regard to the person who makes that statement.

But these logical considerations are not germane to the historicist position. True, to avoid that logical paradox, we should distinguish statements of fact from statements about persons making statements. But this rule does not alter the condition that, through their research, social scientists are implicated in a historical context whether they know it or not. Making that logical distinction will not help them avoid the historical changes to which intellectual interests are subject, or the mutability of truths that are of limited applicability. Our Western society has the special attribute of encouraging the investigation of its own conditions, as well as the detachment of those making these investigations. As a result, the various social science disciplines represent bits of social history. We become social actors when we make man and society objects of our research, for by so doing we help our society to investigate itself. Our purposes as social scientists are at the same time attributes of ourselves as socially and historically active persons. Social scientists may spend only a small part of their time analyzing their own work, but their observations still belong to their interpretation of human action in society.

The historicist approach respects this interplay between subjectivity and objectivity. In doing so, it proceeds from the assumption that people do not act at random, that from the most routine everyday activity to the most specialized performance they act with more or less awareness of what they are doing. As Max Weber has put it, "we shall speak of 'action' insofar as the acting individual attaches a subjective meaning to his behavior— be it overt or covert, omission, or acquiescence."[1] In other words, what people do and how they act makes sense to them and, for the most part, to others.*

Thus, when scholars study men in society, they are interpreting people who are themselves interpreters of what they are do-

---

*Weber's formulation preceded the vast philosophical literature on the meaning of meaning. His rather implicit references were to Goethe's emphasis on the meaning of facts rather than their truth (in his talks with Eckermann); to Dilthey's analysis of subjective experience; to Burckhardt's statement (in his Greek cultural history) that "goals and presuppositions are as important as events"; but perhaps most of all to the analysis of action in the theory of criminal law as analyzed by Gustav Radbruch in his *Der Handlungsbegriff in seiner Bedeutung für das Strafrechtssystem* (1903). Crime is action (or negligence) attributable to an individual, and because criminal law concerns itself with the logic of attribution, Weber as a trained lawyer found the legal approach suggestive. It provided him with an analogue for his own effort to develop a logic of attribution with regard to the sense that people in society make of their action. His definition has an empirical rather than a philosophical thrust which is obscured when his word for sense (*Sinn*) is translated as meaning (*Bedeutung*). Weber's reference was to the ordinary person's understanding, which he shares with others as manifested in language and everyday behavior, leaving aside the multitude of errors, misunderstandings, double meanings, and witting or unwitting distortions which provide so much food for philosophical and psychiatric reflection. This ordinary sense is very close to the statement by W. I. Thomas that "if men define situations as real they are real in their consequences." In Weber's view, there is a social matrix in which ordinary people make sense of their world, but their capacity to do so is also the foundation of individual thought, innovation, and deviation. He would have distinguished his position from that of Imre Lakatos, the philosopher of science, who is concerned with science as a rationally reconstructed world of ideas, a "world of articulated knowledge which is independent of knowing subjects."

ing. But such study itself changes the object, because the people studied are capable of taking into account scholarly analyses of their behavior. In primitive tribes, for example, certain informants who became specialists on their own culture would communicate with Western anthropologists, whose questions they knew already; on occasion they knew even the relevant literature on their own tribe. Moreover, research not only changes the object; research itself does not stand still, because research interests and social change influence each other.

Historicism in American sociology is largely attributable to the influence of Max Weber, even though he has also been interpreted in a rationalist manner. My concern will be to show that Weber's emphasis on subjective meaning is a *modern* phenomenon, occurring in parts of modern literature as well as in the social sciences. For the dominant tendency of the Western tradition has been to search for an objective meaning of history. By "objective meaning" I refer to any view of history which attributes primary significance to forces which originate and work their effects beyond the range of human intention and control. In what follows I sketch five of these objectivist positions which have been especially influential in the West. This overview refers to familiar ideas, but the familiar must be restated if the subjectivist turn of the social sciences and its implication for the history of ideas are to be assessed. This framework is needed if only because the prevailing tendency of the last century has run in the opposite direction.*

II

In the classical Greek view, human affairs are subject to the will and whim of the gods. Good and ill fortune alternate in quite unpredictable ways. Hence, knowledge has the purpose of fortifying the soul and assuaging the envy of the gods. The wise man

*This contrast between the objective and subjective meaning in history is not identical with the old contention between materialism and idealism, although there are of course some points of contact between that contention and the description which follows.

always reflects upon the extreme vicissitudes of fate. In times of the greatest triumph he bears in mind the transitoriness of life; in times of the greatest calamity he reflects upon the unpredictability of fortune, perhaps even the possibility of a renewal. Knowledge is virtue where it helps men attain inner peace in the midst of the fate that is their lot. In this perspective, the mutability of fortunes is the objective meaning of history.[2]

In the eyes of Christian believers, this classical doctrine of eternal recurrence is profoundly impious. Only God can foresee the future, for the existence of the world depends upon His will throughout eternity. Holy Scripture contains God's word, which is vouchsafed to us through faith. Scripture teaches us that God made the world, that in the beginning man committed original sin, that Christ suffered for our sins, and that there will be a day of judgment. Christianity projects the image of a created world in which God's designs are fulfilled and in which, for all their sins, men can hope for a future different from the past. In the Christian view, knowledge—based on faith—involves contemplation of the invisible: God's providence behind the world of appearances and the hope for redemption in the world to come. This speculative reason concerns things that are unchangeable and eternal, like God's act of creation, which contains everything that can exist. Contemplation of God's created world can have an enlightening effect on the whole person, but it is an end in itself, not a means for the invention of new knowledge. Research to invent new knowledge is practical reason, which concerns what is changeable; it is second best because it is a response to man's necessities. Best is speculative reason, contemplation for its own sake. Beyond necessity, apart from the spell of common things, a realm of perfection is believed to exist which belongs to God. Contemplation of that realm is the kind of knowledge which alone can create happiness in the soul of the knower. In this perspective, God's providence is the objective meaning of history, and contemplation of that providence is the highest purpose of knowledge.[3]

There is an irony intrinsic to the history of ideas, as Lovejoy has pointed out.[4] A belief system like the Christian one contains within it certain unsuspected contrary tendencies which in time will destroy the principles of which they are a part. One example is the distinction between speculative and practical reason. For the Christian doctrine to remain intact, speculative reason must rank above practical reason, for the first concerns the unchangeable and eternal order of God, whereas the second deals only with common things. In the early seventeenth century, Francis Bacon argued that speculative reason is barren of results, but that practical reason or science is man's way of conquering the necessities and miseries of mankind. He proposed that knowledge be pursued "for the benefit and use of life," not primarily for the contemplation of what is eternal. But he did not wish to promote one kind of knowledge at the expense of the other; he wished to see the cultivation of both: "Let there be therefore (and may it be for the benefit of both) two streams and two dispensations of knowledge, and in like manner two tribes or kindreds of students of philosophy. . . . Let there in short be one method for the cultivation, another for the invention, of knowledge."[5] Bacon did not yet challenge the accepted belief of his day in the Great Chain of Being; man's use of his mental faculties remained for him a part of God's providential design. But Bacon certainly legitimized the active use of these faculties, which he placed on the same level as the contemplation of divine providence. He helped to initiate that idea of progress which interpreted the advancement of learning as the objective meaning of history.

The idea of the Great Chain of Being is a second example of contrary tendencies within Christian doctrine. Philosophers and poets alike expanded on the theme that in the universe created by God there exists a continuous gradation of beings, "from Infinite Perfection to the brink of dreary nothing," as James Thompson put it in *The Seasons* (1727). Arthur Lovejoy, the historian of *The Great Chain of Being,* has defined the underlying idea as the principle of plenitude: "No genuine potentiality of being can remain unfulfilled, . . . the extent and abundance of the creation must be as great as the possibility of existence and commensurate with the productive capacity of a 'perfect' and inexhaustible Source."[6] Without these assumptions, the work of the Creator would have remained incomplete, a possibility that is incompatible with the attributes of infinite power and wisdom. Yet religious and moral difficulties arise from this logical consistency. In a universe which is and always has been perfect and good, all imperfections are seen as a necessary part of that goodness. "All discord, harmony not understood; All partial evil, universal good," Alexander Pope wrote in the famous verse which ends: "One truth is clear, whatever is, is right." Yet a universe that is perfect and perfectly rational provides no grounds for hope that partial evils can ever be removed. To many thinkers it seemed better to view the world as not entirely rational, which allowed them to retain some hope, than to think of the world "as perfectly rational—and utterly hopeless."[7] The latter conclusion was morally repugnant, and the idea of a created order that was perfect from the beginning was modified to allow for a gradual ascent through an infinity of levels above man in his present state. This conception of the destiny of man as an unending progress harmonized well with the idea of an equally infinite progress through knowledge.

But that reassuring view of man's future did not harmonize at all with the common view of history. As Hegel put it in his *Philosophy of History* (1830), history presents a picture of "restless mutation of individuals and peoples existing for a time and then vanishing."[8] Human interests, passions, and selfish desires cause change, but they disregard law, justice, and morality. On the face of it, history seems to show nothing but decay and corruption. Hegel described this side of history in moving words:

> When we look at this display of passions, and the consequences of their violence; the Unreason which is associated not only with them, but even (rather we might say especially) with good designs and righteous aims; when we see the evil, the vice, the ruin that has befallen the most flourishing kingdoms which the mind of man has ever created; we can scarce avoid being filled with sorrow at this universal taint of corruption; and, since this decay is not the work of mere Nature, but of the Human Will, a . . . revolt of the Good Spirit . . . may well be the result of our reflections. Without rhetorical exaggeration, a simply truthful combination of the miseries that have overwhelmed the noblest of nations and polities, and the finest exemplars of private virtue, forms a picture of most fearful aspect, and excites emotions of the profoundest and most hopeless sadness, counterbalanced by no consolatory result. We endure in beholding it a mental torture, allowing no defence or escape but the consideration that what has happened could not be otherwise; that it is a fatality which no intervention could alter.[9]

Yet in Hegel's view this anguish is superficial, it fails to deal with the heart of the matter; this counterfactual attitude is certainly the most surprising aspect of his position.

Hegel states this other side of the matter in his *Philosophy of Right:*

> It is a sheer obstinacy . . . which does honor to mankind, to refuse to recognize in conviction anything not ratified by thought. This obstinacy is the characteristic of our epoch [the Enlightenment], besides being the principle peculiar to Protestantism. What Luther initiated as faith in feeling and in the witness of the spirit, is precisely what spirit, since become more mature, has striven to apprehend in the concept, in order to [be] free and so to find itself in the world as it exists today. . . . Reason is . . . little content with the cold despair which submits to the view that in this earthly life things are truly bad, or at best only tolerable though here they cannot be improved, and that this is the only reflection which can keep us at peace with the world. There is less chill in the peace with the world which knowledge supplies.[10]

Why does Hegel write with such seeming confidence, despite his own pessimism? One basis for that confidence is the difference between nature and history. Nothing new happens in nature, which consists of ever-recurring cycles like the tides and the seasons. History does not repeat itself in this manner, for it consists of human acts which are always new because men respond with their passions and their reason to ever new circumstances. A second basis is that for Hegel history is primarily a history of thought. Events of the past become known to historians only through documents of some kind which are both evidence of human action and the expression of thought behind that action. And this idea of thought as the arena of history is associated with a third basis for Hegel's confidence. Reason, he believes, is the mainspring of the historical process. This is not an abstract notion. Real people think and act as rationally as they can in the situation they face. But reasoning people are at the same time passionate—always both, never one or the other. Though history may appear solely as the display of passions, this is misleading, for reason uses the passions to achieve what ends it can. A fourth basis for confidence, or at least for hope, is that history ends in the present, not in the future. This tenet of Hegel's is neither as conservative nor as paradoxical as it seems. It expresses the empirical attitude that the historian and the philosopher cannot know the future. They can only know and interpret history up to the present. This does not imply either a glorification of the present or a denial of possible progress in the future; all it means is that the future is not an object of knowledge, but of our hopes and fears.[11] There is more to Hegel's philosophy of history than this short summary can convey, but for present purposes it will be sufficient to add one point which shows how Hegel believed in the objective meaning of history.

The task of philosophy is to comprehend what is, "because what is, is reason."[12] This affirmation expresses both a religious faith and a program of philosophical study. As a descendant of a family of Protestant ministers, Hegel holds that a true believer is reconciled with his God, because for him both nature and history are a revelation of God. Therefore reason must be immanent in the world as its law and essential principle. For religion that reason is an object of faith, for philosophy it is an object of knowledge.[13] After describing the common view of history cited earlier, Hegel writes:

> Even regarding History as the slaughter-bench at which the happiness of peoples, the wisdom of States, and the virtue of individuals have been victimized—the question necessarily arises: to what final aim these enormous sacrifices have been offered?

The concept of providence must be brought to bear upon the historical process so that the ultimate design of the world can be perceived.

> Our intellectual striving aims at realizing the conviction that what was intended by eternal wisdom is actually accomplished in the domain of existent, active Spirit, as well as in that of mere Nature. Our mode of treating the subject is, in this aspect, a theodicy, a justification of the ways of God . . . so that the ill that is found in the world may be comprehended, and the thinking Spirit reconciled with the fact of the existence of evil. Indeed, nowhere is such a harmonizing view more pressingly demanded than in Universal History.[14]

As Karl Löwith has pointed out, Hegel's approach is a curious mixture of degrading sacred history to the level of the secular and exalting the secular to the level of the sacred.[15] But this ultimate ambiguity should not obscure the grandeur of the attempt to justify the ways of God by seeing a universal purpose behind the passionate actions of men who always accomplish ends beyond those they had intended. Hegel believed he had found the objective meaning of history in this "cunning of reason." Yet this attempt to justify the ways of God philosophically gave rise to Marx's attempt to find the objective meaning of history in man's self-realization.

Marx began his work with a critique of Hegel which was at the same time a critique of religion.

> The abolition of religion as the *illusory* happiness of men is a demand for their *real* happiness. The call to abandon their illusions about their condition is *a call to abandon a condition which requires illusions.* . . . The criticism of religion disillusions man so that he will think, act, and fashion his reality as a man who has lost his illusions and regained his reason; so that he will revolve about himself as his own true sun. . . . It is the *task of history,* therefore, once the *other-world of truth* has vanished, to establish the *truth of this world.* The immediate *task of philosophy,* which is in the service of history, is to unmask human self-alienation in its *secular* form, now that it has been unmasked in its *sacred* form.[16]

The true purpose of man, not God's providence, is to be at the center of reality, which man himself fashions after he has regained his reason. At the end of this critique of Hegel's *Philosophy of Right,* Marx summarizes his outlook once more. Germany can be emancipated only, he says, if we adopt the theory that "man is the highest being for man." Man's self-realization is to replace God's providence as the objective meaning of history.[17] But on what grounds does man play so central a role? To answer this question, Marx and Engels had to settle their accounts with their "erstwhile philosophical conscience," a phrase they used to refer to *The German Ideology,* written in 1845–46 but not published until 1932.

In this treatise they start out, they say, from *real* premises rather than arbitrary ones. These premises "are the real individuals, their activity, and the material conditions under which they live, both those which they find already existing and those produced by their activity."[18] Fundamental to this idea of real rather than arbitrary premises is Marx's belief that work is man's basic form of self-realization. Men cannot live without work, hence how they work in society is the main clue to human nature. Men provide for their subsistence by the use of tools; these facilitate their labor and make it more productive. By elaborating and refining these tools, men express themselves, control nature, and make history.

If human labor makes history, then an understanding of the conditions of production is essential for an understanding of history. According to *The German Ideology,* there are four aspects of production, which Marx once again calls "the first premise of all human existence and, therefore, of all human history." These are:

1. the production of the means to satisfy human needs;
2. the satisfaction of one need "leading to new needs";
3. men's propagation of their kind, the relations of the family;
4. the cooperation of several individuals so that each technical mode of production is combined with a mode of cooperation.

It follows that "the multitude of productive forces accessible to men determines the nature of society, hence, that the 'history of humanity' must always be studied and treated in relation to the history of industry and exchange."[19]

There is a logical connection between these four aspects of production. The satisfaction of man's basic needs makes work a fundamental fact of human life, but it also creates new needs. The more needs are created and the more important it is to improve the techniques of production, the more important also is social cooperation, which is a force of production in its own right. The individual's place in social cooperation or the social organization of production indicates the social class to which he belongs. And, as the *Communist Manifesto* (1848) states in its lead sentence: "The history of all hitherto existing society is the history of class struggles." Yet there is an arbitrary premise on which these inferences are constructed, namely, that the necessary conditions of human life are sufficient for the definition of its nature.*

This sketchy survey of the Western tradition suggests that it has nurtured at least five different ideas concerning the objective meaning of history:

1. the classical view of the mutability of fortunes;
2. the Christian view of God's providence as an object of speculative reason based on faith;
3. the belief in progress which consists in the growth of knowledge or the emergence of new forms of life as part of a providential design;
4. God's providential design as an object of philosophical reflection which can reveal the growth of reason and freedom as the unintended by-product of man's passions;
5. man's long-run determination by the material conditions of production throughout the prehistory of all existing societies—together with the irrepressible quest for self-realization—as the foundation of a future society in which the division of labor and human alienation have been eliminated.[20]

III

My understanding of Max Weber's work has been aided by seeing it against the background of this tradition. Weber's primary

---

*The essentialism and arbitrariness of this premise are especially evident in two passages. In *The Holy Family* (1845), Marx writes: "It is not a matter of what this or that proletarian or even the proletariat as a whole *pictures* at present as its goal. It is a matter of *what the proletariat is in actuality* and what, in accordance with this *being*, it will historically be compelled to do. Its goal and its historical action are prefigured in the most clear and ineluctable way in its own life-situation as well as in the whole organization of contemporary bourgeois society." Again, in *The German Ideology*, Marx and Engels write: "Men can be distinguished from animals by consciousness, by religion or anything else you like. They themselves begin to distinguish themselves from animals as soon as they begin to *produce* their means of subsistence. . . . As individuals express their life, so they are. What they are, therefore, coincides with their production, both with *what* they produce and with *how* they produce. The nature of individuals thus depends on the material conditions determining their production." (Tucker, *Marx-Engels Reader*, pp. 105–106, 114.)

interest was not in the history of ideas, yet the prefatory note to *Economy and Society* contains the following telltale remark: "The present work departs from Simmel's method (in his *Soziologie* and his *Philosophie des Geldes*) in drawing a sharp distinction between subjectively intended and objectively valid 'meanings'; two different things which Simmel not only fails to distinguish but often deliberately treats as belonging together." In Weber's view, "objectively valid meanings" are a matter of faith alone. Scholars deal instead with subjectively experienced meanings, though experience is to be interpreted broadly. In many ways, people take for granted the sense of what they do in their everyday behavior. They may hide that sense from themselves or from others (covertness); failure to act may convey their idea or feeling as much as action, sometimes even more so (omission); they may yield to circumstances or personal pressure (acquiescence) and thereby convey a sense of what they are about.

Moreover, Weber's basic definition of sociology distinguishes between action and social action. I repeat the first definition for ease of reference: "We shall speak of 'action' insofar as the acting individual attaches a subjective meaning to his behavior—be it overt or covert, omission, or acquiescence. Action is 'social' insofar as its subjective meaning takes account of the behavior of others and is thereby oriented in its course."[21]

Three aspects of these definitions of action deserve comment. They break and are intended to break with the long Western tradition of a belief in "objectively valid meanings." Obviously, the classical, the Christian, and the progressive views of the world have been widely accepted; and though Hegel seems esoteric, the belief in science which replaced God by Nature is still very popular.

Second, and at a more abstract level, Weber asserts that ideas are manmade and that the social sciences must take this very subjectivity into account. He also asserts that this subjectivity has an irreducably individual component, however socially conditioned our actions are. That is, we are and remain capable of making our own sense of what we do, however much our behavior may resemble that of others. Weber wants to distinguish this capacity from the social actions in which we take the behavior of others into account. He defined action in this way for empirical as well as moral reasons. He believed the ordinary person capable of taking thought of what he is doing. He thought emphasis on this capacity was needed to explain the whole range of conduct from ordinary life to the great innovations of mankind. This was not an argument for free will, for Weber believed that all human actions are caused; it was an argument for asserting that many caused actions are avoidable and are to that extent a matter of choice. Weber also believed that this emphasis represented a value of Western civilization which had universal significance.[22]

Third, Weber was obviously conscious of the fact that the great bulk of human behavior is routine, and that this routine is mediated through the ways we respond to the behavior of others. The great mass of ordinary actions, the prevalence of conformity, the widespread desire to be thought well of by our peers and hence to be sensitive to their expectations: all this comes under Weber's definition of social action, for which David Riesman has coined the felicitous phrase "other-directed behavior." Nevertheless, it is an important part of Weber's scheme to give action and social action, as he defined them, equal weight, so that it becomes an empirical question how these two aspects of ourselves are related in the specific case.

The basic definitions of action are followed by a variety of explanatory comments in Weber's text, one of which should be noted here. Weber states that "in all the sciences of human action, account must be taken of processes and phenomena which are devoid of subjective meaning, in the role of stimuli, results, favoring or hindering circumstances."[23] In other words, in any social situation there are a lot of givens; this was Weber's way of guarding against an idealistic misinterpretation (as he saw it) of his emphasis on subjective meaning. These givens are data which must be taken into account. They are neither lifeless nor nonhuman, nor are they (necessarily) unrelated to human consciousness. Weber emphasized, however, that their admitted importance is not a valid reason for a materialistic interpretation of history. Instead, he took the view that the standpoint from which we, or anyone else, view history is inevitably subjective and inseparable from our own present-day cultural interests. In this way Weber declared his own interest in seeing history in terms of a focus on action that makes sense to the individual by himself, and in his relations to others. He knew that this standpoint itself is a part of history and hence subject to change when its time has run out and when another perspective lays greater claim to our attention and interest. Weber's recognition of this fact makes his work part of the historicist approach to the social sciences.

IV

My own affinity with Weber's work goes well beyond this general point, and here a bit of self-analysis may be in order. Weber belonged to a generation of scholars who, for all their diversity, had one thing in common. They reacted against the materialism of their age, whether it came in the form of Marx's theory of historical materialism, the belief in progress, or the Darwinian struggle for survival. Just consider the years of birth of this remarkable group of men: 1856 Freud; 1858 Durkheim, Mosca; 1859 Bergson; 1862 Meinecke; 1864 Weber; 1865 Troeltsch; 1866 Croce; 1867 Pirandello; 1869 Gide; 1871 Proust; 1875 Jung, Mann; 1876 Michels; 1877 Hesse.[24] I have included literary figures because opposition to materialism and the emphasis on consciousness were obviously not confined to the cultural sciences. Most of these men, perhaps all of them, incorporated into their own work some part of the tendencies they so vigorously opposed. Freud's biological conception of the psyche, Durkheim's advocacy of sociology as a science, and Weber's emphasis on the struggle for survival come readily to mind.

Quite different was the intellectual and historical setting in which I found myself attracted to Weber's work. I was born in 1916 and was seventeen in 1933, when Hitler came to power; I emigrated from Germany in 1938, just after Hitler had annexed Austria and the first great purge trials had been concluded in the Soviet Union. The dominant experience of my youth was not the materialism, but the totalitarianism of the age which arose from a utopian mentality, the belief in man's ability to make over the world in his own image. At the same time, I had been exposed through my father to the teaching of Wilhelm Dilthey, an older member (born in 1833) of that generation of scholars like Weber and Freud who wanted to combine an awareness of human conditioning and limitations with a stubborn emphasis on human consciousness and scientific reasoning.

In the past, the pendulum of the history of ideas had swung repeatedly between the extremes of materialism and idealism, and also of human hope and human despair. Weber, it seemed to me, promised an end to that wavering. He offered an anti-utopian view of the social world which is nevertheless open to its possibilities of development. Karl Löwith characterized the intellectual thrust of Weber's major posthumous work thus: "Even the extreme casuistry of conceptual definitions in *Economy and Society* has not only the meaning to capture and determine reality in definitions, but, at the same time and above all, the opposite meaning of an open system of possibilities."[25] Weber's approach does not lead to a benign view of the human condition, nor does he have all the answers. But his definition of human action encompasses with equal emphasis man's quest for subjective meaning and his compliance with the expectations of others. His definitions of class and status group do the same for man's acquisitiveness and his quest for honor. His definitions of morality do the same for actions guided by a sense of responsibility for the outcome and those guided by a surpassing conviction which disregards all question of consequences. Indeed, his writings reveal polarities of this kind so repeatedly that I have come to think of them as the theoretical core of his work. This conceptual device is quite ancient, and it is not confined to the Western tradition. But in Weber's hands it acquires two meanings of special significance.

One of these consists in a comparative historical perspective used not only as a methodological device, but as a view of man and society. Every human achievement, every social fact or historical situation allows a conceptual formulation only by emphasizing certain properties while neglecting or excluding others. Hence every formulation bears within it the seeds of its own obsolescence. Accordingly, the study of man and society cannot rest content with the observation of any one set of facts without at least noting their cultural, chronological, and other limitations. Sooner or later, such limitations will provoke contrary tendencies, what has been conceptually excluded will reassert itself, and before long new constellations will develop.

If the results of research are to be cumulative, they must be so formulated as to remain open to this eventual obsolescence. In the classical Greek view, the wise man achieves equanimity in facing this mutability of fortunes. A scholar can do no less; indeed he should do more. For him, man and society are objects of inquiry, not objects of contemplation as for the classical philosophers. He must note the given conditions of social facts, whether in the manner of Durkheim's morphology, Weber's "stimuli, results, [and] favoring or hindering circumstances," or Braudel's history of constant repetition and ever-recurring cycles. But having done that, he must also examine the possibilities of action which men have explored time and time again. However difficult to employ in practice, the principle of comparison is indispensable if students of society are not to remain as hidebound by the evidence before them as the concerned actors themselves. The disparity between theory and practice (rather than their unity, as Marx saw it) is important precisely because the freedom to contemplate possible alternatives is often most accessible to those who are not themselves compelled by circumstances.

Weber's use of conceptual polarities is also important because of its anti-utopian orientation. Fascism and communism are two versions of the utopian mentality. However dissimilar in ideology, both assume that man and society are subject to total manipulation. If either racial identity or the organization of production are the ultimate determinants of history, then whoever controls these factors is capable of directing history. In both cases the consequences of utopia have been so abhorrent as to inspire a fundamental distrust of utopianism. Weber's conceptual polarities provide a block against utopian tendencies without downgrading the consideration of alternatives. Such considerations are essential, for this is obviously not the best of all possible worlds, but then neither is it the worst. Hence, differences between democracy and a one-party dictatorship, between a technology used for benign or malignant ends, should be carefully considered rather than obliterated in one apocalyptic vision of the forces of darkness and the forces of light. Utopians set so high a goal for the future that nothing present is worth preserving, and it is this all-or-nothing posture which Weber's approach condemns as self-defeating. By demanding the impossible as the only rational course in a totally irrational world, utopians militate against the possible. For if every human condition has limits and invites or provokes countervailing tendencies, then a utopian society is one without limits and hence without alternatives. Weber notes that aiming for the impossible is sometimes needed to achieve the possible. But his whole work shows that a society without limits is not a possible human achievement.

One corollary following from this observation is to turn to studies of the limits inside which men make, or fail to make, what choices they can. Although I did not begin my own comparative historical research in that way, the purpose of this book is to formulate the intellectual rationale of my work. For that reason I begin the following chapters with a consideration of "men making history" viewed in the historicist framework discussed above. Before one undertakes comparative research, one should formulate the vantage point from which one approaches the subject; as I said earlier, this is one of the preliminaries to any inquiry worth pursuing. I state my position on men making history in sections II and III of Chapter 3.

Section IV requires a different introduction. It summarizes the structural differences between the English, French, German, Russian, and Japanese aristocracies in the years around 1700. At one level, this summary presents conclusions derived from the first part of *Kings or People: Power and the Mandate to Rule* (1978), where I present the historical emergence of divergent sociopolitical structures by focusing on the changing relations between supreme rulership and the landed aristocracy. Here, I present the various results of these historical antecedents. At another level, the contrasts between the social structures of these five countries in the early modern period show the different traditions of aristocratic societies from which the structures of modern societies have emerged. True, one can speak of tradition and modernity in the singular; I have shown that this simple contrast underlies a variety of approaches to the problem of modernization. I am concerned to stress the differences between these rationalistic approaches and the historicist position outlined above and for the further reasons stated at the beginning of Chapter 3.

Three
Embattled Realms

I

Max Weber's generation reacted against the materialism of the age. The next generation, those born around the turn of the century, rebelled against a satiated bourgeoisie and its moralism, and their rebellion was exacerbated during World War I and the Russian Revolution of 1917. For people of my generation in Europe, fascist and communist totalitarianism was the decisive experience of their lives, and this accounts for my emphasis on the study of authority. But emigration to America widened my horizons and extended my interests to problems of modernization.

In the years following World War II, the empires of England, Holland, and France disintegrated. The member states of the United Nations increased from 51 to 142 in a period of thirty years. Most of these new states represented old societies with weak political institutions and little experience in self-government beyond that of tribal rule. Many of the new states, which still remain very poor, are former colonies, and their present situation is partly attributable to conquest and exploitation by the European powers since the late fifteenth century. Between 1500 and 1850, the occupation of Siberia by tsarist Russia represented a similar conquest and exploitation, though Siberia has never been

46

labeled a colony—surely a successful bit of early tsarist propaganda. Today, political order is still precarious in these formerly occupied or still dependent areas which are nevertheless struggling to become independent, even if they are recognized as states.

In asking how the politically and economically leading countries of the modern world had coped with the problem of stabilization and development at an earlier time, it came about that authority, legitimation, and the attributes of a civil society (as distinguished from the state and the military) became central themes in my comparative historical studies.

All writers, from the ancient Greeks to contemporaries like Almond or Wallerstein, agree on the importance of circumstances or prevailing trends in the development of human affairs. Whether we call these conditions fortune, providence, or the organization of production, whether we opt for Braudel's long *durée* or Weber's "favoring or hindering circumstances," every student of society must come to terms with the limitations of human action. The question is merely from what vantage point and in what spirit this common theme is approached. Does it refer solely to climate, geography, and economic conditions, as Braudel and Wallerstein assert? Or does it also include the geopolitical situation of countries, the role of culture in human affairs, and even, on occasion, some outstanding individual? Weber emphasizes these second aspects without losing sight of the first, and this is the position I have adopted in my own studies. I take my motto from de Tocqueville, who observed in one of his letters that each great change of the past has occurred "without having been anticipated by any of the writers in the times immediately preceding these total revolutions." Elsewhere in his correspondence he applies this outlook to his own work.

> I have endeavored, it is true, to describe the natural tendency of opinions and institutions in a democratic society. I have pointed out the dangers to which it exposes men. But I have never said that these tendencies, if discovered in time, might not be resisted, and these dangers, if foreseen, averted. . . . For my part, I wish society to confront [the perils of democracy] like a strong man who knows that danger is before him and must be met, that he may

reach his object; who exposes himself to it without repining, as to a necessary part of his undertaking, and is alarmed only when he cannot see clearly what it is.[1]

Neither Tocqueville's position nor Weber's is tantamount to a "great man" theory, nor does it disregard the large role which circumstances or necessities play in our lives. Their assumption and mine is rather to oppose the unthinking determinism which people take over mistakenly from the natural sciences, or into which they slide unwittingly because they feel helpless and cannot transcend in thought the limitations of their private lives. I believe this transcendance can be achieved in a number of ways, and I shall try to achieve it here in terms of history. Take the case of German fascism. How far are we obliged to trace or justified in tracing its prehistory? During World War II books appeared which sought to make all events since the Lutheran Reformation responsible for National Socialism. Since 1945 writers have been satisfied on the whole with going back only to the German empire since 1871. Still others emphasize the hapless fate of the Weimar Republic. Most explanations of German fascism in terms of some German historical antecedents have a certain plausibility. But a logical contradiction results if we pile such plausible explanations one upon the other and make German fascism "ever more inevitable."

I oppose this construction because partial causes do not simply add up, and a "mounting inevitability" makes no sense. More important, I oppose the construction because to contemporaries the outcome of their actions is uncertain, and at each point the maneuvers and conflicts which will determine the outcome have yet to occur. I want to give back to men of the past the unpredictability of the future and the dignity of acting in the face of uncertainty. In looking back, we observers tend to deprive the past of the future belonging to it because our knowledge of subsequent events misleads us. These are my reasons as a social scientist for having given as much space as I did in *Kings or People* to how social structures emerge from the sequence of events. In what follows, I turn first to an elaboration of this position which emphasizes indeterminacy and the interplay between freedom and fate in human affairs. Following this general discussion, I arrest the flow and uncertainty of events in order to characterize the role of force and of structural elements in history.

II

Men make their own history; but they make it under given conditions, and they become entangled thereby in a fate which is in part the result of other men having made their own history earlier. This sentence encompasses three aspects of our historical experience: given circumstances, action that is historically relevant, and the consequences of this action, which begin as the intended results of what we do but turn unwittingly into seemingly unalterable conditions of our lives.

What do "given circumstances" mean? A comparison of England and Japan answers this question. Both countries are island empires whose history was influenced decisively by their relations with the mainland. This parallel may be superficial, but it is still instructive as a comparative historical description of the differences between the two countries.

England was subject to invasions from the time of the Roman occupation in A.D. 43 to the Norman conquest of 1066, a little more than a millennium. Roman occupation ended during the fourth century A.D., as the frequency of Anglo-Saxon raids and invasions increased. Those raids led eventually to the establishment of many petty kingdoms. In turn, Anglo-Saxon England was conquered by the Danes and shortly thereafter the Normans, leading, for the first time, to centralized rule (at least by the standards of that day) and the virtual expropriation of English-held landed property. Yet, this centralization was compatible with local rule. Under the Romans, local administration had been left in the hands of tribal Celtic authority; in the Anglo-Saxon kingdoms, local affairs were under the shire courts and later the sheriff, though this decentralization was counteracted by the Christianization of England after the late sixth century. At that time, the Christian missions and the local churches they established gave their support to the king's authority, setting a precedent for a balance of local and royal authority that was continued under Norman rule. Following the Norman conquest, that balance was reinforced by the peculiarity that by then the English king and many of his nobles owned land in France as well as England, so that both the king and his vassals were feudatories to the king of France. (Though Normandy was lost in the early thirteenth century, English landholding in other parts of France lasted for three centuries more.) "From the Norman conquest until the seventeenth century, English history moved back and forth between strong assertions of royal authority and strong countervailing tendencies of local autonomy and political representation."[2]

The same cannot be said of Japanese history. The two countries have little in common other than their geographic separation from a continent. Perhaps the most important contrast between them is that in ancient times Japan was not conquered. Instead, the Japanese islands were settled gradually by large kin groups or clans from the mainland which pushed the indigenous population into the outlying areas. Through marriage or fictive kinship ties, through the acceptance of tribute from subordinate extended families and clients, power eventually gravitated in protracted struggles toward the Yamato chieftains. The position of emperor emerged from this ascendance of one clan over its rivals. The emperor became and remained the chief worshipper at the Shinto shrines on behalf of the people, although each clan and family retained its household shrines as well. The continuity of religious ideas in Japanese history from earliest times is impressive, in contrast to the major break with the ancient worship of ancestors brought about by the introduction of Christianity to England. The spread of Buddhism to Japan had no comparable effect; instead it led to the coexistence of ancestor worship and the beliefs underlying Shinto and Buddhist practices.

Following the rise of the Soga clan, families of regents wrested power from the emperor. The Soga and the Fujiwara ruled during six centuries until they were replaced by the Kamakura (1185–1333) and Ashikaga (1338–1573) shoguns, the first strong and the second weak. During the latter part of the Ashikaga shogunate, civil war replaced all semblance of authority. By the mid-sixteenth century a new consolidation of power and authority had emerged, notable especially under the rule of Toyotomi Hideyoshi (1581–1598), who stripped the peasants of their weapons and forced the samurai to reside in castle-towns. Up to this time one could say of Japan that strong assertions of shogunal authority alternated with strong assertions of local autonomy, and that there was no development of representative institutions. There was little balancing between these countervailing tendencies either before or after 1614, when the new centralized rule of the Tokugawa shogunate (1614–1868) was established. In contrast to England, Japan witnessed either a great concentration or a considerable fragmentation of political authority.

Even a fact as apparently unequivocal as the insular location of a country can have quite divergent consequences. Nor do economic or geopolitical conditions have straightforward consequences. The exploitation of the rural population was a feature of Russian history in its Kievan period, as well as under Mongol overlordship, under the Muscovite dynasties, and after the emancipation of the serfs in 1861; and it has continued since the revolution of 1917. In Central Europe, the political fragmentation of the German territories lasted from the breakup of the Carolingian empire in the ninth century to 1871; since 1945 the country has been divided politically on a new basis.

All these diverse circumstances are apparently compatible with many different economic structures. Thus, "given circumstances" mean that there are conditions of long duration which seem to go together with a great diversity of human actions, and which cannot be attributed to any one cause. These conditions are best labeled geopolitical, and they represent the different historical legacies with which the people of any country must cope as best they can. No doubt this is what Marx meant when he wrote that "the tradition of all the dead generations weighs like a nightmare on the brain of the living."[3] He neglected to add that such traditions can be enabling as well as disabling, and that in any case each country must deal with its past.

III

What does it mean that men make their own history? In the comparative study *Kings or People,* I outlined the conditions under which in Western Europe one of our modern political institutions—the idea that rulers are subject to the law—developed. No doubt the earliest antecedents cannot be traced, but it seems sufficient to refer to the controversies surrounding the claims of the Bishops of Rome in the fourth and fifth century A.D. In the West, the bishops were confronted with pagans and heretics who had overrun the Roman empire; in the East they faced the rival spiritual claims of an emerging Eastern Christianity backed by the Byzantine empire. The struggles surrounding the claims made by the bishops lasted for some four centuries. But in 754 the Carolingian regent Pepin, ruler of the Frankish empire after having usurped the royal title in 751, was consecrated "king" and titled "patrician" by Pope Stephen II, who anointed Pepin on behalf of the church. By A.D. 860, the Archbishop of Rheims could say that men of the church like himself had elected the king to govern the kingdom "on condition that [he] observe the laws."[4]

This example illustrates the double emphasis of the lead sentence of this section, that men make their own history, but make it under given conditions. The Bishops of Rome, the Byzantine emperors, and various dignitaries of the church like Boniface or the Archbishop of Rheims, as well as the Merovingian and Carolingian rulers of the Frankish empire, were historical figures. The contentions over the ecclesiastical authority of the Bishops of Rome have been traced in detail and can be summarized as they are in *Kings or People*. But the reference at this level is to men making their own history; and in this case men struggling, arguing, and maneuvering made a substantial difference. Prior to the fourth century, the claims of the Bishops of Rome were much disputed; after the eighth century the ecclesiastical supremacy of the papacy was acknowledged throughout Western Europe. A great historical dispute lasting some four centuries eventuated in a settlement which endured from the eighth century to the Reformation of the sixteenth century, and in Catholic parts of the world which has endured in modified form to the present. Men making their history *have* thereby made a difference. But they also become entangled in the destiny which they and their predecessors helped to shape.

But is "imprisoned" or "entangled" quite the right word? To answer this question, the exercise of power rather than the mandate to rule must be considered. Until the breakthrough to a commercialized economy in the sixteenth century, most societies of the world had some features in common. More than 80 percent of the people lived on the land, as subjects forced to live close to subsistence level. Frequent wars and epidemics slowed population growth but did not inhibit it, though there were exceptions like the Black Plague, which began in 1348 and broke out from time to time thereafter, causing population to stagnate intermittently for some three centuries. Despite such setbacks, the population increased generally at a rate which allowed rulers to maintain relatively large political units and considerable military establishments. One estimate puts the governing class at 1–2 percent of the population, appropriating at least half of society's income above bare subsistence.[5] The vast bulk of the population was constrained by poverty and had little or no influence on the course of events.

Is it also true that the small minority which benefited from this kind of society had little influence on events? At first glance the answer is yes, because of geography and the political configurations associated with geography. England was separated from the continental mainland only by a narrow, easily crossed channel and was subject to many invasions, whereas Japan was separated from the Asian continent by a large sea and was more or less immune to invasions. Russia's political unification was impeded for long periods by attacks from the west, the east, and the south. In the center of Europe, Germany's historical political division was exacerbated by the prolonged effort to unify an empire embracing both Germany and Italy—an example of "given circumstances" arising from prolonged political and military efforts. But there was no way for men to change the English channel and the Japan Sea, or to alter the vast expanse of the Russian steppe.

A second look makes the answer less certain, for geographic location can facilitate action as well as inhibit it. Although political divisions in the center of Europe have lasted a millennium, the two dynasties of the Hapsburg (since 1273) and the Hohenzollern (since 1415) families succeeded in building empires which lasted for centuries out of their widely scattered holdings. In the Russian case, political unification under the Muscovite dynasty took some five centuries to emerge, but after the fourteenth century Russia became an imperial power. Russia has remained unified even after the overthrow of the tsarist regime and the establishment of the Soviet Union. Seen from this standpoint, geopolitical configurations easily outlast changes of the economy, even such major transformations as those from feudalism to capitalism or from capitalism to the collective ownership of the means of production.

However, the history-making actions of men are not confined to such long time periods and to the summit of the social structure. After all, action refers not only to events or deeds, but just as well to creations in technology, science, and art. Emphasis should be given not only to the innovative capacity of men and its world-changing effects, but equally to the dialectic of freedom and constraint which arises from these effects, whether or not this is intended. Weber has reminded us that the power of convention in human life is so pervasive that something new can occur only through man's capacity for innovation. But he has also emphasized the routinization of charisma. This routinization refers in particular to the consequences of human inventions, for at their beginning creative acts allow us much more leeway to act than we are left with by the results of those acts. One need think only of the paradoxes of printing, which is as serviceable to the diffusion of knowledge and enlightenment as of superstition and vulgarization. And there are the paradoxes of modern means of communication, like computers or supersonic flight, which create many new constraints in the very act of overcoming earlier ones. A similar paradox applies to Marxism: it remains a puzzle that a doctrine of human emancipation through the *collective* exploitation of capitalism's productive potential has become rooted in underdeveloped countries, where it is turned into a doctrine of forced industrialization through coercive economic measures. In relation to these and similar transformations, our modern awareness is most adequately expressed if we attend in equal measure to man's history-making innovations and to their unintended consequences—always attending to both and always alert that they may be out of balance. Men make their own history, but the question is whether they will cope with the consequences of their action. To pose this question implies considerable skepticism toward the belief in progress and the theory of evolution that have been prevalent during the past century.

But this discussion, which has been confined to long-run developments and to ruling groups that possess a certain freedom of action, must be supplemented. My earlier statement went too far when I conceded that the bulk of the population has little or no influence on the course of events. This assertion does not take into account that the mass of simple people have a culture of their own, however imprisoned they may be in circumstances beyond their control. Given their low status in society and the exploitation to which they are subject, they have few opportunities of making their voice heard. But they do not deserve on that account "the enormous condescension of posterity" toward the defeated and the silent of which E. P. Thompson has written.[6] The reason for this reservation is not just sympathy for the afflicted. It is rather that the mass of the population is a more or less collective actor in the unfolding of history as are those who lose out in struggles among the ruling few. Sometimes the defeated recoup their fortunes, and sometimes the people at large also rally into action, quite aside from the fact that rulers still have to deal with both groups to make sure of their acquiescence and cooperation. The "condescension of posterity" is inappropriate regarding both the defeated among the upper strata and the lower strata of the population.

IV

In retrospect it always seems as if everything had to develop just the way it did. I call this view the fallacy of retrospective determinism—which looks at the modern world as a victory of the children of light over the children of darkness if we approve of the development, and of darkness over light if we condemn it. But as Herbert Butterfield has observed, it is the *clash of wills* which is necessary for the emergence of the present, and the final result of that clash is unknown to the participants.[7] In this sense, my aim in *Kings or People* was to describe the clash of wills between rulers and aristocrats in each of the countries treated— and in sufficient detail so that the reader gains a vivid impression of the way men make their own history and how in so doing they become entangled in the results of their own actions. I then described the results of these clashes at the summit of the social structure. But to do this, I had to leave the specific contentions at the factual level in order to characterize the problems of the social structure, that is, the recurrent conflicts in the relations between rulers and aristocrats, at a more abstract level.[8]

There are advantages and disadvantages at different levels of abstraction. Every narrative history uses abstractions through its selection of materials. Moreover, narratives close to the events tend to mix different levels of abstraction, whereas abstract treatments separate different levels one from another more easily. Which form of presentation and level of abstraction one choses depends on the purpose of cognition. One can speak of indeterminacy here. Either one analyzes the possibilities of action by examining the sequence of events, or one analyzes social structures by describing their recurrent problems and their comparative results at some arbitrarily chosen time; one cannot do both at the same time. By looking at past events from a contemporaneous viewpoint we create a dynamic picture, or by looking backward at the results we create a static picture. Looking backward always presents an overdetermined depiction of fate; by this perspective we leave out of focus the possibilities of action which existed at the time. I am a determinist only in this methodological sense.

In what follows, the result of the clash of wills at the summit of the medieval social structure will be described in two ways. First the recurrent problems in the relations between rulers and aristocrats are discussed in order to isolate important factors of medieval politics. Second, a comparative situational report is made on the social position of the aristocracy in five countries around 1700, in order to characterize the differential political structure with which these countries entered the modern world of industrial societies.

The purpose of both analyses is structural. I want to specify the framework, the implicit social contract, by which for a considerable period men made their own history. Certain conditions were predetermined by the state of technology, the relations of production, and the material resources of each country, as well as by its geopolitical situation. Such structural analyses say nothing about the options which remained within the framework I describe; these must be left aside for reasons of analytical emphasis. But the question of options examined in the preceding discussion should not be forgotten.

I begin with Max Weber's concepts of patrimonialism and feudalism. The issues of medieval politics can be understood as conflicts and compromises resulting from these logically incompatible principles of rule.

Patrimonialism refers to the management of a large household and estate, either that of the king or that of a major vassal (magnate, aristocrat) under the king. This management is in the hands of the king's or magnate's personal servants, who are maintained as part of the ruler's household and rewarded for their services at his discretion. On this basis, patrimonialism develops as a structure of authority with the expansion of a ruler's personal domain and of his jurisdiction over territories outside that domain. Expansion always implies the increased delegation of authority and, by the same token, the increased complexity of retaining control over deputies or agents. The men who earlier attended the person of the ruler become charged with increased responsibility and receive greater and more permanent rewards for their service. As they rise in the world, they often leave the household and become less permanently dependent upon their master.

The secular and religious position of the ruler provides him with a buttress against this tendency toward greater autonomy. As the patriarchal master of his household and the lord of the domains and territories under his jurisdiction, the ruler possesses absolute secular authority. He exercises that authority by virtue of the consecration which originally authenticated him in his position.

In principle, a ruler cannot deny the religious limitation of his authority without undermining its legitimacy; but the consecration of that legitimacy also justifies the absolute arbitrariness of his will. The combination of a ruler's arbitrary will with his submission to a "higher law" is a defining attribute of traditional domination, as Max Weber uses that term. Hence, the attempt to limit the arbitrary will of a ruler by an appeal to the absolute sanctity of a transcendental power recurs periodically. On the other hand, types of patrimonialism vary, depending upon the prevailing idea of supernatural sanction and the institutions through which a ruler's penultimate authority is consecrated.

The issues of medieval politics concern in good part the conditions of royal administration. On the basis of the economic resources derived from his domains and his vassals, each ruler seeks to enlarge the territories under his authority. In these efforts, he necessarily relies upon those who can aid him financially and militarily. But such aid from local notables enhances their own power as well as his. Therefore, secular rulers typically seek to offset the drive toward local autonomy by devices that increase the personal and material dependence of such notables upon the ruler and his immediate entourage. In this setting, every demand by a ruler for increased revenue and military service can be countered in principle, though often not in fact, by countervailing demands for increased privileges in return for the greater services to be performed. The balance or imbalance achieved in these contentions are the self-imprisoning results of men making their own history.

Feudalism refers to the mutual recognition of rights of a ruler and his territorial lords. (Because the ruler and his lords also hold absolute authority over their own domains, patrimonial and feudal elements of rule usually coexist.) The vassal swears an oath of fealty to his ruler and thus acknowledges the obligation to serve him. In return, the ruler grants a fief to his vassal, or confirms his existing possessions as a fief. Where the feudal element predominates, these grants include a guaranteed immunity: within the territory held in fief a vassal is entitled to exercise certain judicial and administrative powers. Where the patrimonial element predominates, such powers remain parts of the ruler's jurisdiction.

Considered comparatively, the feudal type of authority is, again, a generic phenomenon. Under primitive conditions of communication, the ruler of a large territory is obliged to delegate the direct exercise of authority to household officials who are becoming more independent, or to local notables who are becoming more dependent. Typically, feudal vassals are small territorial rulers in their own right, exempt from obligations which are specifically excluded under the reciprocal understandings of fealty. In Western European feudalism, the relations between a ruler and his vassals were consecrated through an affirmation of rights and duties under oath and before God, a practice which presupposes the idea of a transcendent system of justice. This idea was reinforced not only by appeals to a higher moral law but, more directly, by the political power and canonical authority of the church, which reinforced the vassal's consciousness of his rights against the rights of other vassals and the rights of the ruler.

The contentions between the patrimonial and the feudal principle of authority result in a system of divided and overlapping jurisdictions, or immunities. Each jurisdiction accords positive public rights which entitle particular privileged persons and corporate groups to exercise a specific authority and to levy fees or tolls for that exercise. In the aggregate such jurisdictions constitute a political community, which may be held together firmly or precariously, depending on the momentum of past events, external circumstances, the personal capacity of the participants, and the vicissitudes of the political struggle.[9]

What was the structure of politics in England, France, Prussia, Russia, and Japan around the turn of the seventeenth century? The ongoing clash of wills is arbitrarily arrested in order to obtain a situational report; to that degree the answer describes "end-results" of post medieval politics. Such a report, whether extended or abbreviated, is closer to the events than the abstractions just discussed, but only proximately so. It still takes imagination to see the transition from kings to people in the constellation of issues around 1700.

In *England,* the "glorious revolution" of 1688 had settled upon the constitutional principle of the king-in-parliament as the sovereign authority of the country. In the resolutions passed by the House of Commons in January, 1689, the ousted King James II is accused of having broken "the original contract between king and people; and by the advice of Jesuits . . . having violated the fundamental laws." The resolutions also declare that it is "inconsistent with the safety and welfare of this Protestant kingdom to be governed by a Popish Prince."[10] No one questioned the principle of monarchical government, provided the king-in-parliament exercised authority in conformity with the "original contract between king and people." This was the quasi-populist theory. The practical problem was how to avoid anarchy when locally based powers were strong and the monarchy weak. England had had too many ineffectual rulers; the ideological defense of absolute monarchy was counterproductive, as in the case of Thomas Hobbes; the armed forces were weak; and the judiciary provided support for local interests. Conspiracies and rebellions had prevailed for three generations during the seventeenth century.

The other side of the coin was a picture of growing strength. Population increased, foreign and domestic trade as well as internal water transport advanced, and, at the local level, the landed gentry and a mercantile elite combined economic prosperity, a strong social and political position, and nationwide economic links. People at this local level and in Parliament were suspicious of the royal court, jealous of their independence, and ready to quarrel about rights of property. There were, as J. H. Plumb writes, a

> myriad marks of status, of possession, of profit: stewards of hundreds, precentors of cathedrals, beadles of corporations. Usually, these offices were held for life and they all enjoyed standing and status within the community they adorned; most of them carried a vote. Such freeholds bred independence, truculence, a willingness to fight and litigate that bordered on neurosis, and yet when they conglomerated, as in the universities, the cathedral cities, and the Parliamentary boroughs, they could build up into formidable heaps of political influence.[11]

And that influence did not remain at the local level.

Electoral contests became numerous not only between rival local factions, but between local notables representing "the country" and the crown with its agents. With women, children, and laboring poor excluded, the estimate of two hundred thousand electors out of a population of six million is impressive. The size of the electorate was only one of many contested issues. As the electorate increased, techniques of pressure and persuasion proliferated at local and national levels. In the end, the revolution of 1688 was provoked by James II's specific attacks on the military establishment and, in the name of toleration, on the universities and on the Anglican monopoly in the Church. But the revolution became universally popular when the king attacked the acknowledged leaders of society in their own local neighborhoods. In the short run, this threat to the local basis of political power led not only to the overthrow of the king, to a bill of rights that buttressed the position of Parliament, and to a new monarchy, but also to further political instability.

> What the Revolution did was to confirm the authority of certain men of property, particularly those of high social standing, either aristocrats or linked with the aristocracy, whose taproot was in land but whose side-roots reached out to commerce, industry, and finance. And their authority was established not so much because Parliament became a continuous part of government but because they settled like a cloud of locusts on the royal household and all the institutions of executive government. For these prizes, they fought each other—at least for thirty years or so after the Revolution—after which Walpole sliced up the cake for them and reduced their quarrels to bickering about the crumbs.[12]

Thus, in the short run, parliamentary supremacy intensified many local quarrels by giving them national "representation." But in the long run, political instability was curbed because an oligarchy of men of property and standing, with ties to the land and economic ties throughout the country, managed to settle on a distribution of positions in the royal household and the executive government. The point to note is that the men who occupied the highest positions in Parliament, at court, and in the government were at the same time the social and political leaders of the countryside in which their estates were located.

In *France,* the Estates-General had not developed into a representative body like the British parliament. Its existence depended upon royal summons, and its last meeting had occurred in 1614. The ascendance of the French monarchy had been assisted by the impoverishment of the French nobility during the Hundred Years' War with England (1338–1453). Then, monarchy *and* nobility were weakened by the religious wars between Huguenots and Catholics which lasted from 1562 to 1598. France was split into a Huguenot party, intent on gaining civic recognition for the Reformed faith, and the party of the Counter-Reformation led by the dukes of Guise. The French king negotiated and fought with both parties. (The Guises' relation by marriage with the French and Scottish royal houses made the French religious wars part of an international contest as well.) Strong monarchical rule was reestablished by Henry of Navarre, who came to the throne in 1589 as Henry IV, a Huguenot who converted to Catholicism in 1593 and sponsored the charter of religious toleration, the Edict of Nantes of 1598. Though the king was assassinated in 1610, the French monarchy gained ascendance thereafter under a succession of regents (Cardinals Richelieu [1624–1642] and Mazarin [1642–1661]), and especially under Louis XIV [1661–1715].

This ascendance was difficult to achieve, though probably not so difficult as in England. Pierre Goubert writes of France that in practice the monarchy rested on a series of contracts made

> with the different units of which France was composed: provinces, cities, ecclesiastical foundations, social classes and even economic groups such as the trade guilds. All these contracts left to each group its own liberties and privileges and no one saw anything out of the way in their existence side by side with submission to the king. Provinces, cities, foundations, groups, orders and estates were all faithful subjects of the king, but with their own privileges.[13]

Under these conditions, centralized rule often remained on paper. but under Louis XIV, from 1661 on, it became a reality more often than not—at the center of affairs, at any rate. The sovereign courts of France, the *parlements,* were instructed in 1673 to register royal edicts forthwith; they could still address petitions to the king, but his word was law. The officers of finance were either bought out by the government or replaced by the *intendants,* new provincial governors who took over the assessment of the tax (*taille*). The highest ranks of the nobility, including princes of the blood, were excluded from the councils of government in favor of middle-class careerists entirely dependent on the will of the king. Louis XIV's lavish court society at Versailles had the political purpose of forcing the nobility's personal attendance. Nobles could win favors only by personal petition, often impoverishing themselves in the process. Those who stayed at home were subjected to searches of their titles; this

calculated subordination of recalcitrants could lead to their de-
motion and provided an indirect means of taxation besides.

True, a semblance of the old institutions remained. The
Estates-General were not formally abolished; they were simply
not summoned. The *parlements* retained their right to petition,
but only after they had registered the king's edicts. The old provincial governors were kept at court, where they could be
watched, and their former functions were taken over by the *intendants*. The towns retained some forms of self-government but
were increasingly controlled by the *intendants,* and in many a city
the election of the mayor was superseded by the purchase of that
office. The point to note is not simply that France lacked a representative body like the British Parliament. It is rather that the
men who occupied the highest positions at court were forced to
reside there or nearby if they hoped to obtain the king's favors.
Yet they were excluded both from the important positions of
government and from the social and political leadership of the
countryside in which their estates were located. At the same
time, men of middle-class origin who won the king's favor and
occupied the truly important positions had no effective ties to the
countryside. Hindsight would suggest that the later troubles
which led to the transition from kings to people had their origin
in this systematic removal of the French nobility from its roots in
the countryside and from its (already weakened) position of local
and national leadership. The bourgeois careerists who replaced
aristocratic careerists in the king's service were similarly objects
of royal manipulation.

The reign of Louis XIV lasted from 1661 to 1715. For half of
that fifty-four year period, his affairs prospered: France became
the dominant power of Europe and Versailles its cultural and
ceremonial center. The decline from this eminence can be dated
from the revocation of the Edict of Nantes in 1685, which helped
to unite the greater part of Europe against France. Of one million French Huguenots, perhaps some two hundred thousand fled
the country, and their emigration aided the economic development of Protestant countries while helping to impoverish France.
From 1688 to 1697, Louis XIV was at war against the League of
Augsburg; from 1702 to 1713 he was engaged in the War of the
Spanish Succession. In 1711 and 1712 his son, his eldest grand-

son, and his eldest great-grandson died. By the time Louis XIV himself died in 1715, the debts of France amounted to 430 million livres, with several years' revenue mortgaged in advance. Before as well as after 1715, the financial requirements of the court and the exigencies of war prompted the French government to forego the direct administration of affairs by selling both offices and rights to collect taxes, a less direct but more immediately lucrative method. The financial needs of the crown led to ever new compromises, in which various privileged groups and financiers advanced money to the crown in exchange for privileges that could be exploited at the long-run expense of the crown and the country. After the death of Louis XIV, weaker rulers and a great ascendance of privileged groups followed. These groups not only increased their exploitation of the country, but through the high courts of *parlements* often frustrated the exercise of royal authority. At one level, they were merely insisting on their ancient and not so ancient rights; at another, and quite unwittingly, they were set on a collision course with the monarchy.[14]

Brief as these sketches are, my situational reports on Prussia, Russia, and Japan must be briefer still. In *Prussia,* the ascendance of the Hohenzollern house over the landed estates was aided by several dynastic marriages and, more inadvertently, by side effects of the Thirty Years' War (1618–1648), which weakened the political and economic position of the landed aristocracy. Frederick William, the Great Elector (1640–1688), managed to triple total revenue during his reign and raise his standing army from 4,500 to 30,000 men. Shortly afterward, in 1704, the Prussian Landtag gave its last formal assent to the amount of revenue that would be assessed in rural areas. Thereafter, the Prussian rulers dominated their militarized state almost unopposed, though they unstintingly supported the economic and administrative predominance of the aristocracy in the countryside. In Prussia, the aristocracy was "domesticated," not by court service as in France, but by militarism. Most cities became garrison towns. A standing army and regular taxation helped to undermine the earlier independence of estate assemblies. On royal initiative, old-fashioned regional patriarchalism was replaced by the central bureaucracy and its agents. Subsequently, a division of tasks was achieved between central and local administration whereby the latter was largely put in the hands of the landed aristocracy. Not even hindsight can discover anything in the Prussian constellation around 1700 with regard to a possible transition from kings to people. First intimations of such an occurrence had to await the cultural developments of the eighteenth century and Prussia's defeat by Napoleon in 1806. One should add to these events the emergence of an educated state bureaucracy in the late eighteenth century, for those circles were receptive to the ideas of law and constitutional reform.

In *Russia,* the prolonged ascendance of the Muscovite dynasty led to the subjugation of all rival principalities by the reign of Ivan III (1462–1505) after Mongol power in the east and Lithuanian power in the west had weakened. Around 1300, Muscovy extended over 47,000 square kilometers; by 1600 it had reached 5,400,000 square kilometers. Before 1462, the country had been subjected to 133 invasions, and between 1500 and 1700 it had been engaged in 136 years of war. Certainly the ever-recurring military engagements had a great deal to do with the subordination of the landed aristocracy to tsarist authority. By the reign of Peter the Great (1689–1725), that subordination had culminated in the *mestnichestvo* system, which stipulated the rank of aristocratic families by the length of their service to the tsar, not, be it noted, by the length of their residence and landed tenure in the countryside. Two-thirds of all male aristocrats had to serve as army officers for twenty-five to thirty years; the remainder were obliged to serve at court and/or in the administration; the management of landed estates belonging to the aristocracy was largely in the hands of bailiffs. As a result, all local administration in towns and villages was under the direct authority of the tsar's officials. Nowhere, not even in France, was the separation of the landed aristocracy from its estates as complete as it was in Russia.

Again, hindsight cannot discover any intimations of a development away from absolute tsarist authority, though perhaps one qualification should be added. With all authority concentrated in the hands of the tsar and with the whole society organized for war, the weak link of the *political* structure was the problem of succession. (There were other weaknesses which are not considered here.) In 1718, Peter's son Alexis was tortured to death in his father's presence on a trumped-up charge of conspiracy. In

1722, Peter proclaimed the tsar's right to appoint his own succesor, but in 1725 he died without having done so. The futility of such an unbridled assertion of authority became evident thereafter, as six of the succeeding reigns involved usurpations, assassinations, and an increasing role by the Moscow guard regiments in struggles over the throne. The next strong ruler, Catherine II (1762–1796), came to the throne after having at least condoned the assassination of Peter III (1762), her husband and predecessor. Yet Catherine's reign was the first during which ideas of a constitutional monarchy were discussed; and the landed aristocracy were formally exempted from their lifetime obligation to serve in the army or at court. Other reforms followed in the nineteenth century, but none of these moves toward emancipation were harbingers of a transition from autocracy.

In *Japan,* the Tokugawa shogunate consolidated its central authority by reducing or confiscating the lands of 218 out of 245 daimyo, affecting an estimated 75 percent of the area under cultivation in 1651. With the preponderance of their house assured, the Tokugawa regime secured internal peace by combining isolation—the Western missions were expelled and Japanese foreign travel prohibited—with an internal security system. This system was based on the personal loyalty of the servant to his master and was reinforced by a strict order of rank, a ubiquitous police force, and the frequent taking of hostages to guarantee loyalty. But within the system a remarkable degree of local autonomy was achieved. The villages had earlier been freed of their immediate landlords (under Toyotomi) and given considerable autonomy in exchange for total demilitarization and the annual taxes in rice for which they were jointly responsible. The samurai now constituted a class of rentiers with a guaranteed, if circumscribed income and the exclusive right to bear arms; at the same time they were obliged to reside in the castle-town of their respective domains (*han*), ready to serve their daimyo. The daimyo were complete masters within their family domains; the entire population was at their service. Most of them were "improving landlords" because their wealth and prestige depended upon the prosperity of their domain. The daimyo were obliged to maintain a residence in Edo (Tokyo), and they or members of their family had to be present (usually on a rotating basis) to perform duties at the shogunal court. This personal presence guaranteed continuing loyalty in the provinces.

The five countries reviewed differ strikingly in terms of their relation between the landed aristocracy and the national community. These differences represent the basic structures with which the several countries entered the modern world. There is no single type of traditional society, but many types. The conditions around 1700 represent for me an arbitrarily arrested result of long-term historical antecedents, as well as a prefiguration of developments which have taken place since then. This conclusion can be stated in a few sentences.

In England, the social and political preeminence of the aristocracy at the local level was directly related to its national prominence. The king-in-parliament system which possessed sovereign authority over the country also represented the country. Regardless of many disturbances and much class antagonism, local people felt that the landowning aristocracy were the proper people to run the affairs of the community and the country. Where inequality is a fact of daily life, it is often accepted in principle, even though there are sporadic protests against particular instances of injustice and exploitation.

In France, the prominence of aristocrats at court was the sine qua non of their social status, which depended on the king's personal favor. Those who did not attend upon the king were threatened with examination of their titles to land. This required presence at court entailed separation from the management of the landowner's estate. National prominence was, therefore, often incompatible with personal ties to the local community. Such prominence required conspicuous consumption; bailiffs often cheated the landowners; and the owners purchased income-producing offices from the government. Meanwhile, royal officials governed and exploited the countryside. As Tocqueville observed, the aristocracy still enjoyed its privileges, but it no longer performed its customary functions.

In Prussia, landed aristocrats were "domesticated" through lifetime military service. Recruited in their teens, they would return to their estates only when they were fifty or older. Their families' local prominence was supported by the monarchy not only because county administrators (Landräte) were recruited from their ranks, but because young peasants were recruited into the army—so that personal relations on the estates resembled relations between officers and men in active service. Tensions occured frequently between royal officials and landed aristocrats, but the overriding fact of Prussian society was the king's supremacy as ruler and commander-in-chief. This regime was crowned with success by the unification of the German empire in 1871, and the three-class suffrage instituted then accurately reflected the subordination of the people to a patriarchal regime.

In Russia, the lifelong military service of the landed aristocracy continued for the most part even after the emancipation of the nobility in 1762. Russian landed nobles were similar in many respects to their Prussian colleagues, but the tsarist government employed its own officials (rather than aristocratic recruits from the local area) to govern the provinces. In effect, the tie between landowners and peasants (serfs in Prussia's eastern provinces and Russia) was broken in France and Russia but maintained in England and Prussia. Moreover, the formal emancipation of the Russian nobility in 1762 meant that many young aristocrats joined the ranks of the disaffected by taking seriously the enlightened ideas with which Catherine II had dabbled in the interest of an improved image abroad. In the revolt of 1825, in the debates surrounding the emancipation of the serfs in 1861, and in the subsequent agitation accompanying the industrialization of tsarist Russia, Russian aristocrats were split into defenders and opponents of the regime. But neither group had contact with the peasants on their estates, who were under the jurisdiction of tsarist officials. The Russian aristocracy was part of a militaristic regime; and it should be remembered that serf emancipation in 1861, the revolution of 1905, and the revolution of 1917 each followed a major military defeat.

Finally, in Japan, the samurai were separated from the land in the late sixteenth century, whereas their lords were all-powerful in their own local domains. But when it came to national affairs, even the daimyo were subject to controls that effectively precluded their participation in the shogunal government—except on a ceremonial level which indicated their ultimate subordination. Nothing in this constellation suggests even the beginnings of a transition from shogunal to popular rule. Yet it is worth considering that, a century and a half later, the Meiji restoration was initiated in some of the leading *han* among a group of reform-minded samurai. These men eventually managed to meet the threat of Western intrusion by inducing their lords to jointly "return" their whole domains to the emperor, from whom all authority nominally derived. From this self-sacrificing, and selfish, act the movement toward Meiji constitutionalism developed.[15]

It is not customary to think of landed aristocrats when one refers to "the people"; but then, we are heirs to a populist tradition and are no longer accustomed to older meanings of the terms we use. Up to the early modern period discussed here, the laboring poor of countryside and town were not recognized as participants in the existing political communities. As Ernest Barker has pointed out, government could not be distinguished from private property, family relations, and social rank. The affairs of the country were confined to persons of standing in society, a group which included church dignitaries and members of the urban patriciate.

This age of inherited inequality is past, and so is the legal system which supported it. Government and even the private exercise of authority have become separated from property, family, and rank. The laboring poor have become citizens, recognized participants in the political process and equals under the law, however much they continue to suffer the disabilities of low rank and poverty.

Four

Industrialization, Ideologies, and Social Structure

The comparative sketch of the historical situation around 1700 described a world in which inequality was taken for granted. In these aristocratic nations of old, as Tocqueville described them,

> the poor man is familiarized from his childhood with the notion of being commanded; to whichever side he turns his eyes, the graduated structure of the society and the aspect of obedience meet his view. Hence in those countries the master readily obtains prompt, complete, respectful, and easy obedience from his servants, because they revere in him not only their own master, but the class of masters. He weighs down their will by the whole weight of the aristocracy. He orders their actions; to a certain extent, he even directs their thoughts. In aristocracies the master often exercises, even without being aware of it, an amazing sway over the opinions, the habits, and the manners of those who obey him, and his influence extends even further than his authority. . . .

This chapter is a further revision of a lecture originally published in *American Sociological Review*, 24 (October 1959), 613–623, and republished in Reinhard Bendix, *Work and Authority in Industry* (Berkeley: University of California Press, 1974), pp. 436–450. The lecture was given on the occasion of the MacIver Prize, awarded by the American Sociological association in 1958.

> Thus although . . . the master and servant are placed at an immense distance on the scale of human beings by their fortune, education and opinions, yet time ultimately binds them together. They are connected by a long series of common reminiscences, and however different they may be, they grow alike. . . . The master gets to look upon his servants as an inferior and secondary part of himself, and he often takes an interest in their lot by a last stretch of selfishness.[1]

In Tocqueville's view it followed that as a result of this long-enduring structure of inequality, servants develop a pride, virtue, and honesty of their own, feelings of self-respect which pertain to their condition of service because at a great remove they identify themselves with the distinction of their master.[2]

As the descendant of an ancient family of masters, Tocqueville had great insight into this way of life; but, as he emphasized in a letter, he had few illusions about it. On the contrary. He began his great work on democracy in America with the idea that the rise of equality was the master trend of Western history. The Crusades and the English civil war had decimated the nobility and divided their possessions. Municipal corporations had introduced institutions of liberty into the heart of feudal monarchy. Firearms had equalized noble and foot soldier on the field of battle. Printing and the mail had brought resources and knowledge to the minds of all classes. And Protestantism had proclaimed that all men are created equal under God.[3] Yet these master trends of world history had done little in bridging the great gulf dividing masters from servants, employers from workers, until the precepts of contractual agreement had replaced the conventions of status.

Where contract becomes the prevailing relation between persons, this formal equality of condition

> turns servants and masters into new beings. . . . [Now] men are constantly changing their situation; there is still a class of menials and a class of masters, but these classes are not always composed of the same individuals, still less of the same families; and those who command are not more secure of perpetuity than those who obey. As servants do not form a separate class, they have no habits, prejudices, or manners peculiar to themselves; they are not remarkable for any particular turn of mind or moods of feeling.

They know no vices or virtues of their condition, but they partake of the education, the opinions, the feelings, the virtues, and the vices of their contemporaries; and they are honest men or scoundrels in the same ways as their masters are. . . .

At any moment a servant may become a master, and he aspires to rise to that condition; the servant is therefore not a different man from the master. Why, then, has the former a right to command, and what compels the latter to obey except the free and temporary consent of both their wills? Neither of them is by nature inferior to the other; they only become so for a time, by covenant.[4]

The contrast between the two conditions is striking. Though it is always true that masters and employers are rich, whereas servants and workers are poor, under conditions of inequality masters and servants are at times able to consider one another as superior and inferior extensions of themselves. Between them, superiors and inferiors *share* a consciousness of rank. On the other hand, under conditions of contract, employers and workers are equals under the law, but they have little or nothing in common. A family feeling can bridge the vast gap between aristocrats and their servants, but there is no sense of like-mindedness other than the pursuit of individual advantage between employers and workers. A great crisis in human relations occurred when relations based on status were replaced by agreements based on contract.

Tocqueville is nowhere more eloquent than in his description of this transition.

But what shall I say of those sad and troubled times at which equality, . . . after having been introduced into the state of society, still struggles with difficulty against the prejudices and manners of the country? The laws, and partially public opinion, already declare that no natural or permanent inferiority exists between the servant and the master. But this new belief has not yet reached the innermost conviction of the latter, or rather his heart rejects it; in the secret persuasion of his mind the master thinks that he belongs to a peculiar and superior race; he dares not say so, but he shudders at allowing himself to be dragged to the same level. His authority over his servants becomes timid and at the same time harsh; he has already ceased to entertain for them the feelings of patronizing kindness which long uncontested power always produces, and he is surprised that, being changed himself, his servant changes also. He wants his attendants to form regular and permanent habits, in a condition of domestic service that is only temporary; he requires that they should appear contented with and proud of a servile condition, which they will one day shake off, that they should sacrifice themselves to a man who can neither protect nor ruin them, and, in short, they they should contract an indissoluble engagement to a being like themselves and one who will last no longer than they will.[5]

Tocqueville wrote this diagnosis of disrupted social expectations with an eye to the conditions leading up to the French Revolution. But the spread of equalitarian ideas was not confined to France or to revolutions. The commercialization of land, labor, and capital which gained momentum especially in eighteenth-century England was at least as important as the revolution in spreading the idea of equality among people who had always been excluded from the political process and who were now being uprooted from their traditional occupations as tenants and servants. Displaced from the land and crowding into towns in search of employment, they had lost their customary habits and had yet to acquire new ones.

Conditions of work in the early factories were not only inhumane by our standards, they were brutal and chaotic even by the standards of that day. The manufacturers of the late eighteenth century were not accustomed to managing a work force, just as their employees were not accustomed to laboring in these poorly organized work places. What Tocqueville wrote of masters and servants in France applies equally to England: "the master is ill-natured and weak, the servant ill-natured and intractable; the one constantly attempts to evade by unfair restriction his obligation to protect and to remunerate, the other his obligation to obey."[6] This was the atmosphere in which employers made use of the prevailing patriarchalism of the day, perhaps modeled after aristocratic notions of the past but now applied to very nonaristocratic conditions. Here is John Stuart Mill's vivid evocation of this view in 1848:

The lot of the poor, in all things which affect them collectively, should be regulated *for* them, not *by* them. They should not be required or encouraged to think for themselves, or give to their own reflection or forecast an influential voice in the determination of their destiny. It is the duty of the higher classes to think for them and to take the responsibility of their lot, as the commander and officers of an army take that of the soldiers composing it. This function the higher classes should prepare themselves to perform conscientiously, and their whole demeanor should impress the poor with a reliance on it, in order that, while yielding passive and active obedience to the rules prescribed for them, they may resign themselves in all other respects to a trustful insouciance, and repose under the shadow of their protectors. The relation between rich and poor should be only partially authoritative; it should be amiable, moral, and sentimental; affectionate tutelage on the one side, respectful and grateful deference on the other. The rich should be *in loco parentis* to the poor, guiding and restraining them like children. Of spontaneous action on their part there should be no need. They should be called on for nothing but to do their day's work, and to be moral and religious. Their morality and religion should be provided for them by their superiors, who should see them properly taught it, and should do all that is necessary to insure their being, in return for labor and attachment, properly fed, clothed, housed, spiritually edified, and innocently amused.[7]

I have described Tocqueville's and Mill's rendition of the way men of "wealth and command" around 1700 viewed the working people upon whose labor these landed aristocrats and new middle-class entrepreneurs depended for their fortune and way of life. This was the starting point of my *Work and Authority in Industry* (1956, 1974), in which I examined managerial ideologies which justified the authority of superiors over subordinates. In this chapter I am concerned with the historical and theoretical significance of managerial ideologies. In the sections which follow I turn to the ideological changes which have occurred during the past two centuries in Anglo-American and in Russian civilization. Then, section IV deals with the problem of bureaucratization in industry and in particular with the differences between totalitarian and nontotalitarian forms of subordination.

I

What is the historical significance of managerial ideologies? Ruling groups including the ruling groups of developing industrial societies have always sought to give reasons for their good fortune, as well as for the ill fortune of those subject to their authority. Everywhere, industrialization involves the organization of enterprises in which a few command and many obey. I believe that the ideas developed for the many by or on behalf of the few are a clue to an understanding of industrial societies. For such ideas can promote the social cohesion of a class, justify their good fortune in their own eyes, facilitate communication, help resolve the dilemmas of organization with which men in command must deal on a daily basis, and also actually help persuade workers that the distribution of rewards in society is fair.

Ideas may do any of these things only proximately, or not at all. The legitimacy of an industrial society depends, at least in part, on the persuasiveness of these ideologies. Entrepreneurs—managers and others who direct the organizations of industrial societies—have made use of managerial ideologies time and again. These people, who play an important role in modern society, may be deceived by ideas, but they also think they know what they are doing. These are the reasons why I believe such ideas are worth examining over time and in a comparative perspective.

Historically, ideologies of management became significant in the transition from a pre-industrial to an industrial society. The authority exercised by employers was recognized as distinct from the authority of government. This was a novel experience in eighteenth-century England and elsewhere in Western Europe because in the past there had been little or no distinction between governmental authority and the high status bestowed by wealth, family position, and social rank. But the entrepreneurs of an emerging industrial society were more often than not "new men," rather than members of the old ruling class buttressed by tradition. These changes in social structure were reflected intellectually in a theoretical separation between government and society. The discipline of sociology originated during this period. Society, under the impact of the French Revolution, came to be conceived in terms of forces independent from, as well as antagonistic to, the formal institutions of the body politic. Some early elaborations of this key idea enable us to perceive the historical significance of ideologies of management.

The authority of employers rests on the acquisition of property, which eighteenth-century philosophers made the conceptual basis of the social order. In Rousseau's view, that order can be and ought to be based on a general will which presupposes that the individual acts for the whole community. In such a society, as George Herbert Mead has pointed out, "the citizen can give laws only to the extent that his volitions are an expression of the rights which he recognizes in others, . . . [and] which the others recognize in him."[8] This approach provides a model for a society based on consent, so that the power of rule-making is exercised by all and for all. This foundation of society upon a "general will" was directly related to the institution of property. As Mead has stated, "If one wills to possess that which is his own so that he has absolute control over his property, he does so on the assumption that everyone else will possess his own property and exercise absolute control over it. That is, the individual wills his control over his property only in so far as he wills the same sort of control for everyone else over property."[9] Thus, the idea of a reciprocal recognition of rights specifically presupposed the equality of citizens as property owners.

This implication gave pause to some eighteenth- and nineteenth-century philosophers. They noted that the reciprocity of rights among property owners based on freedom of contract does not apply to the relations between employers and workers. As early as 1807, Hegel formulated the problematic nature of this relationship in a manner which anticipates the modern psychology of the self, just as Rousseau's "general will" anticipates the sociological analysis of interaction. Hegel maintains that men come to a recognition of themselves through a process whereby each accepts the self-recognition of the other and is in turn accepted by him. That is, each man's sense of identity depends upon his acceptance of the identity of others and upon their acceptance of him. In Hegel's view, this reciprocity is lacking in the relation between master and servant. The master does not act toward himself as he acts toward the servant; and the servant does not do toward others what his servitude makes him do against himself. In this way the mutuality of recognition is destroyed, and the relations between master and servant become one-sided and unequal.[10]

In Western Europe, this inequality of the employment relationship coincided with the ideological and institutional decline of

traditional subordination. Yet while the old justifications of subordination crumbled and new aspirations were awakened among
the masses of people, their experience of inequality continued or
became worse. I have referred to Tocqueville's diagnosis of this
problem. The master no longer recognizes any responsibilities
towards the servant, but he wants him to be obedient and content. In effect, the master wishes to enjoy the age-old privileges
without acknowledging any concomitant obligations. Meanwhile,
the servant rebels against a subordination which is no longer a
divine obligation and is not yet perceived as a contractual one.
Tocqueville wrote,

> Then it is . . . that [in] the dwelling of every citizen . . . a secret
> and internal warfare is going on between powers ever rivals and
> suspicious of each other. . . . The reins of domestic government
> dangle between [masters and servants], to be snatched at by one or
> the other. The lines that divide authority from oppression, liberty
> from license, and right from might are to their eyes so jumbled
> together and confused that no one knows exactly what he is or
> what he may be or what he ought to be. Such a condition is not
> democracy, but revolution.[11]

In the nineteenth century, men like Hegel and Tocqueville
pointed out that the spread of equalitarian ideas was causing a
transition in the relations between masters and servants. This
transition can be called a crisis of aspirations. Servants "consent
to serve and they blush to obey. . . . [They] rebel in their hearts
against a subordination to which they have subjected themselves. . . . They are inclined to consider him who orders them as
an unjust usurper of their own rights."[12] As a consequence, most
European countries witnessed the rise of a "fourth estate," which
struggled against existing legal liabilities and for basic civil rights,
above all the right to suffrage. In a parliamentary debate on
Chartism, Disraeli remarked that this struggle was invested with
a degree of sentiment usually absent from merely economic or
political contests. To the extent that such complex movements
can be characterized by a common denominator, this sentiment
referred, I think, to the workers' quest for a public recognition of
their equal status as citizens.[13] Where this and other civil rights
became accepted, such recognition compensated for the contin-

ued social and economic subordination of the workers and thus assuaged the crisis of aspirations. Moreover, the political utilization of these civil rights could lead to a recognition of basic social rights which today is embodied in the institutions of social welfare characteristic of many Western democracies.[14] The initial crisis of aspirations continued, on the other hand, where civil rights were rejected or where their acceptance was postponed for too long, leading either to an eventual revolutionary upheaval, as in tsarist Russia, or to a more or less damaging exacerbation of class-relations, as in Italy and France.

My hypothesis is that the break with the traditional subordination of the people gave rise to a generic problem of many industrial societies.[15] The question of nineteenth-century Europe concerned the terms on which a society undergoing industrialization will incorporate its newly recruited industrial work force into the economic and political community of the nation. Ideologies of management are significant because they contribute to each country's answer to this question. In England the workers were invited to go start their own businesses if they did not wish to obey; in Russia they were told that their subordination was less onerous than it seemed because their own superiors were also servants of the almighty Tsar.

II

What are the theoretical implications of my hypothesis? Ideologies of management can be considered indexes of the flexibility or rigidity with which the dominant groups of such countries as England and Russia were prepared to meet the challenge from below. This preparedness or collective tendency to act is analogous to the concept of character structure in the individual: it can be defined as an "inner capacity" for recreating similar lines of action under more or less identical conditions.[16] The ideologies of management which reflect this "inner capacity" naturally provoke new challenges, and these in turn lead to new managerial responses, so that at the societal level a replication occurs of the action-reaction process so typical of interaction among individuals.

An analysis of this process must deal with those explicitly formulated ideas that are as close as possible to the collective experience of employers and workers. This social philosophizing for the ordinary man as a participant occurs at a level somewhere between his attitudes as an individual and the sophisticated formulations of the social theorist. Such philosophizing is exemplified by what Andrew Ure wrote in his *Philosophy of Manufacturers* (1835), or by what the publicity men for General Motors say in their pamphlet *Man to Man on the Job* (1946). But the serious analysis of such documents is at variance with the prevailing tendency to dismiss them as obviously biased and hence unworthy of consideration on their own terms. Marx, it is recalled, reserved some of his choicest invective for his characterization of Ure's book, and in this respect he was a forerunner of the intellectuals born in the 1850s and 1860s. Freud, Durkheim, Pareto, and others shared with Marx the search for some underlying principle or force that could explain the manifest beliefs and actions making up the external record of individual and collective behavior.[17] Many writers of that generation were less interested in what a man said than in why he said it. Accordingly, ideologies of management could be dismissed because they *merely* express a class interest, or because they do not reveal the *real* attitudes of the employers.

Modern social science owes to this intellectual tradition many important insights, but also many of its aberrations. Where the phenomena of the social world are treated merely as the reflection of "hidden forces," speculation easily becomes uncontrolled, with the result that observable evidence is dismissed as "irrelevant" or "uninteresting" on theoretical grounds. The difficulty is familiar in Marx's theory of history, which encouraged him to treat whole series of facts as epiphenomena—such as the "false consciousness" (Engels) of the workers, which was bound to be superseded in the course of history. Similarly, the Freudian approach tends to devalue a behavioristic study of social life because it deals with the appearance rather than the underlying motivations of social action. In inexpert hands all of these approaches lead to a cavalier construction of the evidence which can always be more easily imputed to the "underlying determinants" than analyzed in detail on its own ground.

Yet human experience occurs at this phenomenological level—and the analysis of managerial ideologies illustrates that such study can also provide an approach to our understanding of the social structure.[18] The managerial interpretations of the authority relationship in economic enterprises, together with the workers' contrast-conception concerning their collective position in an emerging industrial society, constitute a composite image of class relations which has changed over time and which differs from nation to nation. This aspect of the changing social structure can be studied by examining each ideological position in terms of its logical corollaries as these relate to the authority of the employers and, in a wider sense, to the class position of employers and workers in the society. Where these corollaries create major problems for the interests of the group, as prevailing opinion defines those interests, the development of tensions and perhaps of change, ideological and institutional, can be expected.[19]

Such ideologies, and this is the second level of analysis, are in part means for running an organization efficiently, in part expediential rationalizations for the problems confronting the entrepreneur, and in part the result of historically cumulative response patterns among social groups. Ideologies are formulated through the constant interplay between current contingencies and historical legacies. As Marx put it in a statement to which I alluded earlier, "men make their own history, but they do not make it just as they please; they do not make it under circumstances chosen by themselves, but under circumstances directly found, given and transmitted from the past."[20] Accordingly, ideologies of management can be explained *only in part* as a means to an end and as rationalizations of self-interest; they also result from the legacy of institutions and ideas which is "adopted" by each generation much as a child "adopts" the grammar of its native language. Historical legacies are a part of the social structure: they should not be excluded from the social sciences, which focus attention upon the persistence of group structures and the unanticipated consequences of conscious social action.

III

At the inception of industrialization in England, an ideology of traditionalism prevailed. John Stuart Mill called it "the theory of dependence," according to which the laboring poor are children who should not be allowed to think for themselves, who must obey and show deference to their superiors, and who in return will be protected against the vicissitudes of life.[21] This interpretation of authority assumes that the dependence of the poor and the responsibility of the rich are the valid moral rules of the social order. In the course of industrial development, these ideas were gradually modified. As the responsibility of the rich was increasingly rejected by the advocates of laissez-faire, the dependence of the poor was turned from an inevitable into a self-imposed fate. As it was "demonstrated" that the rich cannot care for the poor without decreasing the national wealth, it was also asserted that by abstinence and exertion the poor can better their lot. The same virtues which in the eighteenth century were extolled so that the lowly would not aspire above their station were praised by the middle of the nineteenth century because they enabled man to raise himself by his own efforts.

In England, and even more in America, this praise of effort led toward the end of the nineteenth century to an apotheosis of the struggle for existence. A militant language was applied to the relations between employers and workers. Riches and poverty merely reflected differences of ability and effort. The employer's success was evidence of his fitness and as such justified his absolute authority over the enterprise. This assertion of authority has a clear-cut meaning only so long as most managerial functions are in the hands of one man. The idea becomes ambiguous as the use of expertise in the management of enterprises increases and the managerial function becomes subdivided and specialized. Yet the idea of the employer's absolute authority over his enterprise coincided with the "scientific management" movement, which sought to give him expert advice on what to do with that authority. It can be suggested, therefore, that the doctrines of Social Darwinism gradually lost their appeal in part because changes in industrial organization gave rise to a changing imagery of men in industry. From the Gilded Age to the 1920's, workers and managers were self-evident failures or successes in a struggle for survival in which they were the recalcitrant objects or the exasperated originators of managerial commands. Today they have become individuals-in-groups whose skills must be improved and allocated systematically and whose productivity must be maximized by appropriate attention to their psychological makeup. Thus, over the past two hundred years, managerial ideologies in Anglo-American civilization have changed from the "theory of dependence" to laissez-faire to Social Darwinism and, finally, to the "human relations" approach.

In the Russian development there is also the assertion of paternal authority and of childlike dependence, couched in much the same language as in England. But in Russia this ideology of traditionalism was a very different thing from what it was in England because of the tsar's assertion of supreme authority over all the people. This authority remained intact regardless of how many privileges the tsar granted to landlords, and regardless of how rarely he interfered in fact with the use and abuse of these privileges. Ideologically, the tsar maintained his preeminence through repeated assertions concerning his paternal care and responsibility for all of "his" people. Through repeated petitions and sporadic revolts the people used this tsarist claim in order to obtain redress for their grievances against landlords and employers. Finally, because of the early centralization of authority under the Muscovite rulers, the whole distribution of wealth and rank among the aristocracy turned upon the competition for favors at court and hence reinforced the tsar's supremacy.[22]

During the second half of the nineteenth century, this pattern of tsarist autocracy had far-reaching consequences. The dislocations incident to the emancipation of the serfs (1861) and the development of industry brought in their train assertions of absolute authority by the employers, efforts of the workers to organize themselves, and sporadic attempts of the government to regulate the relations among them. The government, though ostensibly acting on an equitable basis, in fact supported the employers against the workers. Much of this is again broadly familiar from the English experience; but Russia's historical legacies prevented the shift in ideology which has been described for England. As long as tsarist autocracy remained intact (roughly until 1905), neither the rejection of responsibility by the tsar and the ruling strata nor the demand for the self-dependence of the workers developed on a significant scale. Instead, the tsar and his officials continued to espouse the traditional ideology of patriarchal tutelage. Officials supported the employers but frequently criticized their abuses. At the same time, especially after the revolution of 1905, the tsarist government sought to curb these abuses by granting the workers a circumscribed right to organize trade unions and to conduct strikes for purely economic objectives.

Tsarist autocracy was undermined in the Russian revolution of 1905 and overthrown in 1917. Although vast changes were brought about by the revolutions, the managerial ideology of tsarism lived on in modified form. Tsarist officials had regarded employers and workers as equally subject to the will of the tsar; loyal submission to that will was the mark of good citizenship. In theory, Lenin believed that all workers were equal participants in the management of industry and government; their loyal submission to the Communist party represented their best interest and expressed their sovereign will. The logic of Lenin's, as of the tsarist, position is that under a sovereign authority the same person or organization can and should perform both subordinate and superordinate functions. For example, Soviet labor unions approach the ideal of workers' control of industry when they are called upon to participate in the management of industry. But they also function in a managerial capacity when they inculcate labor discipline among their members under the authoritative direction of the Communist party.

Ideologically, this position is defended on the ground that the party represents the historical interests of the proletariat against the short-run interests of individuals and factions. In such an orientation there are still traces of tsarist autocracy, for all wisdom and responsibility reside in a small group or, indeed, in one man, who, like the tsar, knows better than private persons what is the good of all and who can only wish the well-being of the people. But there is also an important difference. The leaders of the Russian revolution were faced with the task of developing self-discipline and initiative among workers if a suitable industrial work force were to become available.[23] They proceeded to inculcate these qualities by the direct or indirect subordination of everyone to the discipline of the Communist party. This policy continued the tsarist tradition by making all matters the object of organizational manipulation rather than of individual initiative.

But Soviet rule also represents a break with the past. It is engaged continually in mobilizing the entire population.

IV

Since the eighteenth century, Anglo-American and Russian civilizations have witnessed a growing managerial concern with the attitudes as well as the productivity of workers. It is possible to relate this change of ideology to a large number of the developments which comprise the transition from an early to a mature industrial society. The changing structure of industrial organizations is only one of these developments. Yet the bureaucratization of economic enterprises is of special importance for any attempt to interpret the difference of fact and ideology between a totalitarian and nontotalitarian form of subordination in economic enterprises. Bureaucratization is also especially suitable for a study of authority relations in industry, because it involves processes that are directly comparable in two such different civilizations as England and Russia. This choice of focus deliberately eschews a comprehensive theory of society in favor of selecting a problem which, if suitable for comparative analysis, will also lead to an analysis of social structures. For if comparable groups in different societies confront and, over time, resolve a common problem, then an analysis of their divergent resolutions will reveal the divergence of social structures in a process of change.[24]

Problems of a systematic management of labor come to the fore where the increasing complexity of economic enterprises makes their operation more and more dependent upon an *ethic of work performance*. This ethic involves a degree of steady intensity of work, reasonable accuracy, and a compliance with general rules and specific orders that falls somewhere between blind obedience and unpredictable caprice. Where personal supervision is replaced by impersonal rules the efficiency of an organization will vary with the degree to which these attributes of work performance are realized, and this realization is part of the ongoing bureaucratization of economic enterprises. That is to say, management subjects the conditions of employment to an impersonal systematization, whereas the employees seek to modify the implementation of the rules as their personal interests and their commitment (or lack of commitment) to the goals of the organization dictate. There is no more effective means of organizational sabotage than a letter-perfect compliance with all the rules and a consistent refusal of the employees to use their own judgment. "Beyond what commands can effect and supervision can control, beyond what incentives can induce and penalties prevent, there exists an exercise of discretion important even in relatively menial jobs, which managers of economic enterprises seek to enlist for the achievement of managerial ends."[25] In the literature on organizations this exercise of discretion by subordinates is known by a number of terms: Veblen called it the "withdrawal of efficiency"; Max Weber referred to it as the bureaucratic tendency toward secrecy; Herbert Simon might call it the "zone of nonacceptance." I have suggested the phrase "strategies of independence" to get away from the negative connotations of these other terms. By the exercise of discretion, subordinates may serve to achieve, as well as to subvert, the goals of an organization.

The great difference between totalitarian and nontotalitarian forms of subordination consists in the managerial handling of this generic attribute of all authority relations. The historical legacies of some Western countries have encouraged management to presuppose the existence of a common universe of discourse between superiors and subordinates, and this presupposition is related to the successful resolution of the crisis of aspirations. From the evangelism and the tough-minded laissez-faire approach of eighteenth-century England to the latest refinement of the human relations approach, managerial appeals have been addressed to the good faith of subordinates in order to enlist their cooperation. Whether such good faith actually existed is less important than that such appeals were made, though it is probable that in England and the United States large masses of workers in one way or another have accepted managerial authority as legitimate even if they were indifferent to, or rejected, the managerial appeals themselves. In Russia, on the other hand, historical legacies did *not* encourage management (under the tsars) to presuppose the existence of a common universe of discourse between superiors and subordinates. From the time of Peter the Great to the period of rapid industrial growth in the last decades preceding World War I, managerial appeals were addressed to the workers' duty of obedience toward all those in positions of authority. Whether or not the workers actually developed a sense of duty, the appeals presupposed that they had not. Accordingly, officials and managers did not rely on the good faith among their subordinates, but attempted instead to eliminate the subordinates' strategies of independence.

This managerial refusal to accept the tacit evasion of rules and norms or the uncontrolled exercise of judgment is related to a specific type of bureaucratization which constitutes the fundamental principle of totalitarian government. In such a regime the will of the highest party authorities is absolute in the interest of their substantive objectives. The party may disregard not only all formal procedures by which laws are validated, but also its own previous rulings; and where norms can be changed at a moment's notice, the rule of law is destroyed. Totalitarianism also does away with the principle of a single line of authority. Instead of relying on an enactment of laws and on the supervision of their execution from the top, totalitarian regimes use the hierarchy of the party in order to expedite and control at each step the execution of orders through regular administrative channels. This is the major device by which such regimes seek to prevent officials from escaping inspection while compelling them to use their expertise in an intensified effort to implement the orders of the regime. A totalitarian government is based, therefore, on two interlocking hierarchies of authority. The work of every factory, of every governmental office, of every unit of the army or the secret police, as well as of every cultural or social organization, is programmed, coordinated, and supervised by some agency of government. But it is also propagandized, expedited, criticized, spied upon, and incorporated in special campaigns by an agency of the totalitarian party, which is separately responsible to the higher party authorities.

The rationale of this principle of double government can be stated within the framework of Max Weber's analysis of bureaucracy. An ideally functioning bureaucracy in his sense is the most efficient method of solving large-scale organizational tasks. But this is true only if these tasks involve a more or less stable orientation toward norms which seek to maintain the rule of law and to achieve an equitable administration of affairs. These conditions are absent where tasks are assigned by an omnipotent *and* revolutionary authority. Under the simulated combat conditions of a totalitarian regime, the norms that govern conduct do not stay put for any length of time, although each norm in turn will be the basis of an unremitting drive for prodigies of achievement. In response, subordinates will tend to use their devices of concealment for the sake of systematic, if tacit, strategies of independence. They will do so not only for reasons of convenience, but because the demands made upon them by the regime are "irrational" from the viewpoint of expert knowledge and systematic procedure.[26] The party, on the other hand, seeks to prevent the types of concealment that make such collective strategies possible by putting every worker and every official under maximum pressure to utilize his or her expertise to the fullest extent. This is the rationale of a double hierarchy of government, which places a party functionary at the side of every work unit in order to prevent concealment and to apply pressure. The two hierarchies would be required, even if all key positions in government and industry were filled by party functionaries. For a functionary turned worker or official would still be responsible for "overfulfilling" the plan, and the new party functionary would still be charged with keeping that official under pressure and surveillance.[27]

In this way, totalitarianism replaces the old system of stratification by a new one based on criteria of activism and party orthodoxy. The ethic of work performance on which this regime relies is not the product of century-long growth, as in the West, but of material incentives and of a political supervision that seeks to prevent evasion from below as well as from above. For example, the collective "bargaining" agreements of Soviet industry are in fact declarations of loyalty in which individuals and groups pledge themselves publicly to an overfulfillment of the plan, whereas the subsequent organization of public confessionals, the manipulation of status differences between activists and others, the principle of collective leadership, and further devices seek to maximize performance and prevent the "withdrawal of efficiency." The individual subordinate is surrounded almost literally. Aside from ordinary incentives he is controlled by his superior and by the party agitator who stands at the side of his superior, but he is also controlled "from below" in the sense that the social pressures of his peer group are manipulated by party agitators and their agents. This institutionalization of suspicion and the consequent elimination of privacy are justified on the ground that the party "represents" the masses, spearheads the drive for Russian industrialization, and leads the cause of world communism.

The purpose here has been to state the case for a comparative analysis of social structures which pays attention to the historical continuity of societies, as well as to the concatenation of group structures and deliberate, self-interested action in the process of social change. In lieu of abstract considerations, I have tried to make this case by analyzing some implications of ideologies of management in the course of industrialization.

The changes in ideologies of management during the past two centuries in Anglo-American and in Russian civilization are similar insofar as they can be characterized as an increased managerial concern with the attitudes of workers which presumably accounts for their differential productivity. But this overall similarity coincides with a fundamental divergence. In Western civilization the authority relations between employers and workers has remained a more or less autonomous realm of group activity even where the human relations approach has replaced the earlier individualism. In Russia, the employment relationship has been subjected throughout to a superordinate authority which regulates the conduct of employers and workers and which can transform superiors into subordinates (or, more rarely, subordinates into superiors) when government policies seemed to warrant such action.

Authority relations in economic enterprises as a universal attribute of industrialization lend themselves to comparative analysis, and these comparisons are historically important. For example, ideologies of management became significant when the equalitarianism of property owners brought to the fore by the French Revolution, and by the legal codifications which followed, was contrasted with the inequality of the employment relationship. A heightened awareness of this inequality coincided with the decline of a traditional subordination of the lower classes and hence with a rise of aspirations for social and political as well as for legal equality. In England, these demands for equal rights of citizenship on the part of the lower classes eventuated in a painful but peaceful reconstitution of class relations; in Russia, the same demands were rejected and finally led to the revolutions of 1905 and 1917.

The comparative study of ideologies of management is of theoretical as well as historical interest. Such ideologies can be considered indexes of a readiness to act which, together with the ideological responses of other groups, can provide us with a clue to the class relations of a society. Ideologies, it is assumed, are an integral part of culture, which should be analyzed on its own terms as an index of the social structure, much as the neurotic symptoms of an individual are analyzed as an index of his personality. It is further assumed that such ideologies are expediential rationalizations of what are taken to be the material interests of a group, but that such rationalizations tend to be circumscribed by the historical legacies which are a part of a country's developing social structure.

Although ideologies of management can be treated as a clue to class relations, it is also worthwhile to relate them to other aspects of the social structure. One such aspect which is especially suitable for a comparison of totalitarian and nontotalitarian regimes is the fact that all industrial enterprises undergo a process of bureaucratization, and all bureaucracy involves the use of discretion in the execution of commands. Comparison between the Anglo-American and the Russian traditions shows that managerial appeals have differed in terms of whether they have presupposed the good faith of subordinates. Where that presupposition has not been made, the drive for industrialization takes the specific form of a double hierarchy of government which is designed to apply maximum pressure on subordinates and to forestall their evasion of commands by supplementing executive with political controls at every point in the chain of command.

The processes of both English and American, as well as Russian industrialization have been marked by bureaucratization; and bureaucratization certainly threatens the development of initiative.[28] But the Soviet case also illustrates that this threat can provoke countermeasures. One might speak of an institutionalization of initiative in the totalitarian party, and one can speculate that the dynamic drive of the Soviet regime might be jeopardized by too much relaxation of the Cold War which appears to justify that drive.

In 1980–81, these considerations have acquired new and unexpected relevance. The events in Poland have shown that, especially in the satellite countries of Eastern Europe, the institutionalization and monopolization of all initiative by the ruling Communist party are limited in certain ways. These limits had become visible already in the liberation movement of Hungary of 1956 and in the "Prague spring" of 1968. But these partial movements of independence from the Soviet Union were confined to the leading strata and could be suppressed with relative ease through military intervention by the Warsaw Pact countries under Soviet leadership. Polish developments since 1980 have added a new dimension to these precedents; it is difficult to assess their consequences in 1982 and it will perhaps be difficult for a considerable time thereafter. In Poland, the trade union Solidarity with its ten million members has contested the legitimacy and the leadership monopoly of the Polish Communist party. The movement began in mid-1980, and its challenge has proved decisive, for by December 1981 a military dictatorship had been imposed under pressure from the Soviet Union. When two independent organizations—a nationwide trade union and the Communist party—claim to represent the working class and the nation, the monopoly of a single-party system is breached. It remains an open question whether the current suppression of Solidarity will remain effective (as seems likely), and if so whether in Poland and perhaps elsewhere in the Soviet empire military rule will replace (or perhaps alternate with) the Communist party as the supreme authority. This is the new context in which the comparative analysis of managerial ideologies will remain an important task with reference to the Soviet Union and its satellites.

New contexts for such analyses have appeared also in the industrial societies of the West. Doubts have increased whether technical and scientific advances are always progressive. Questions have arisen as well with regard to the political integration of the "second proletariat," that is, of ethnic minorities and foreign workers.

Five

The Citizenship of the Lower Classes

I

In England, the early phase of industrialization was accompanied by the emergence of a non-agrarian labor force. This is true of a number of industrializing countries but not all. One need only think of Russia, where some industrial production began in villages, or of America, where some industrial workers had labored in factories before their immigration. Today, in many underdeveloped countries, an urban work force is already in existence before industrial enterprises are established. In these cases, rural overcrowding and migration to the cities in search of a better life precedes industrialization. Nevertheless, it can be said that countries undergoing rapid industrialization face major social and economic changes, and the burden of these changes falls regularly upon the lower strata of the population.

A proper assessment of these changes may never be entirely successful. With reference to northwestern Europe, for example, there is a general understanding that a customary hierarchy of social rank existed prior to the spread of secular ideals of equality and the development of modern industry. It seems likely that a tradition of personal command and obedience gave rise to reciprocal expectations. These implied, in principle at least, that ser-

91

vants could expect a secure subsistence in return for willing subordination. Inequalities of long standing can generate customary acceptance or usage, even if these do not mean satisfaction. But information about the lower ranks of society is difficult to assess, and retrospective judgments vacillate. Examples of obedience are cited as easily as examples of insubordination or movements of protest—hardly a basis for firm conclusions. Nor are resistance, social protest or even violence synonymous with revolution. Moreover, assessments of this evidence are not extricated easily from current political ideas. Many generalizations about the lower strata of the past are placed at the service of contemporary political goals which the lower strata "must" or "should" bring to pass. Finally, intellectuals have tended to attribute their own social ideals to workers and peasants.

In light of such considerations, only this much can be said in general about the lower strata of a pre-industrial society. It seems probable that these lower strata have experienced a rather modest level of expectation. Poor people want a decent standard of living and the respect of their neighbors. Also, poverty, heavy physical labor, and plain coercion leave only occasionally enough energy to hope for more than a steady and decent level of life. None of this should be allowed to minimize either the psychological burden of poverty or the constant stream of invidious gossip with which the exploited relieve their feelings—or yet the frequent dreamers among them who think up schemes whereby the last shall be first. Even so, it makes little sense to impute present-day revolutionary expectations or hopes to the past. It does make sense to speak of an unwritten social contract as the basis of the old regime. At any rate, one cannot speak of revolution without assuming the existence of such a contract. Social protest within the framework of the status quo should be distinguished from the destruction of the status quo, even when the transition from one to the other is gradual. Marx was probably right when he wrote that the ruling ideas of an age are the ideas of the ruling class. The lower strata are typically influenced by such ideas. It is another question whether the same generalization also applies to the intellectuals of the old regime.[1]

The "honest poor" occupied an altogether low and subordinate place, but a recognized place, before the age of equality.

This assumption is plausible because individuals from the lower strata lost that place time and again and became moral and legal outcasts, even in the opinion of their own class. Such outcasts were individual cases or occurred in large numbers; one estimate of these "dishonest people" in the societies of medieval Europe put them at one-quarter of the lower strata. But whatever their number, the social category of outcasts suggests that conventional opinion distinguished between them and the "honest poor."[2] And where that distinction was accepted generally, it makes sense to say that in the early period of industrialization the lower classes lost not only their place in society, but the social recognition that went with it. It follows that societies undergoing a process of industrialization frequently face as one of their major problems whether and how citizenship will be extended to the new industrial work force.

This problem arises because traditional subordination was synonymous with some claim to protection by one's superiors and strict exclusion from public affairs. Once workers and peasants were emancipated from their age-old personal subservience, they lost what protection they may have enjoyed and became exposed to market fluctuations of wages and prices. In the late eighteenth century no one said that the people's exclusion from public affairs had ceased. But the situation had changed. The laboring poor began to protest the consequences of market fluctuations by contending that their new working conditions deprived them of their ancient rights. In their agitation for the right to organize and bargain collectively, workers blended this idea of ancient rights with their claim to a minimum of social justice under the new conditions. Workers contribute to society, are entitled to a fair reward, and must be allowed to take what steps are needed to assert their equal rights as citizens under the law. Lorenz von Stein described this situation in 1846:

> Labor was deprived of the power to provide the individual with the goods he needed for his livelihood. Awareness of this fact is indeed the specific reason for the workers' estate creating that opposition to the entrepreneurial estate which is peculiar to our time. On the one hand, this opposition is based on the idea of the higher destiny of the individual and hence of the worker as well.

On the other, that opposition is based on the worker's recognition that under present conditions work is essentially dependent on machines and the wages which result cannot satisfy his claims. It is this awareness which creates the proletariat.[3]

Class consciousness and its incipient revolutionary tendencies are, therefore, associated with the early phase of industrialization. That is, as a society industrializes it tends to be jeopardized by revolutionary impulses which arise from the demands for social recognition of the lower strata. This early class struggle concerns the old rights of peasants and workers. The issue is the public recognition of ordinary labor as a social value, either within the social order undergoing industrialization or in a new social order which can guarantee such recognition.

In this perspective, the class struggle of industrial societies is a matter of social recognition after the earlier hierarchical order has been superseded, in part at least, by a system of formal equality. In theory, every person is a citizen like every other— before the law and in the marketplace. But in practice laborers find themselves at an economic disadvantage at every turn. Persons without means cannot help themselves on their own; hence they turn for assistance to others in the same position. But when they do so during the early phase of industrialization, they typically find that they are denied the right to form mutual aid societies or trade unions. To achieve public recognition of that right is the first object of the class struggle. Only after the right to form organizations has been obtained can the struggle for social recognition become concerned with collective bargaining agreements on a regular basis. Today we know that still further problems arise, once those earlier struggles have resulted in industrial relations of mutual accommodation.

II

The industrialization of the modern economy "began" in England around the mid-eighteenth century, and this development became an incentive for the industrialization of other countries.

In a general way, industrialization can be used simply as a synonym of sufficiently rapid economic growth so that by 1960, for example, countries with one-third of the world's population produced about 80 percent of the world's income. But in the narrower sense industrialization refers primarily to the economic results of technical progress. New knowledge is applied in the process of production so that the amount of goods and services produced per unit of labor, capital, and raw materials increases rapidly.

Economic growth of this kind has political repercussions for two reasons. First, industrialization raises the questions if and how the government by its policies helps to promote that growth. Government participation presupposes a more or less efficient bureaucracy. Second, industrialization leads to, and depends on, the rapid development of a free labor market. Peasants and workers become emancipated from their previous dependence upon landowners and craft guilds, but now they must bear all the risks associated with their new independence. Where it functions well, a free labor market presupposes an economy and a state capable of providing work, a level of wages which permits a decent standard of living, and public assistance to those without means during periods of economic decline or personal incapacity. In this idealized sense industrialization cannot be separated from bureaucratization and public welfare measures. But in fact one cannot assume either the efficiency of government or its ability and willingness to provide welfare. In effect, workers and peasants are compelled to become politically active in order to enlist the government's efforts in their own behalf. This presupposes a political mobilization which can be facilitated by the development of a free labor market, provided a favorable cultural and political environment develops as well.

Two descriptions from around the middle of the last century describe the political consequences of industrial mobilization. For an understanding of the extension of citizenship to workers, it is useful to compare the two. One description is by John Stuart Mill.

Of the working men, at least in the more advanced countries of Europe, it may be pronounced certain that the patriarchal or paternal system of government is one to which they will not again be subject. That question was decided when they were taught to read, and allowed access to newspapers and political tracts; when dissenting preachers were suffered to go among them, and appeal to their faculties and feelings in opposition to the creeds professed and countenanced by their superiors; when they were brought together in numbers, to work socially under the same roof; when railways enabled them to shift from place to place, and change their patrons and employers as easily as their coats; when they were encouraged to seek a share in the government, by means of the electoral franchise. The working classes have taken their interests into their own hands, and are perpetually showing that they think the interests of their employers not identical with their own, but opposite to them. Some among the higher classes flatter themselves that these tendencies may be counteracted by moral and religious education; but they have let the time go by for giving an education which can serve their purpose. The principles of the Reformation have reached as low down in society as reading and writing, and the poor will not much longer accept morals and religion of other people's prescribing.[4]

Mill's formulation certainly overestimated the readiness of English property owners to accommodate the demands of the lower strata, for workers had yet to engage in prolonged struggles in order to gain the franchise.

Still, it seems that in comparison with Marx, Mill's diagnosis of his time was rather closer to the truth as we know it now. One can document, of course, that Marx was as aware as Mill of the spread of literacy among workers, the appeals of Protestant divines, the new geographic mobility, and above all the concentration of workers in the same workplace. Both writers leave no doubt that a class struggle was occurring and that English workers were finding a new independence. But Marx's main emphasis was on strikes, coalitions, trade unions, and the development of political parties, that is, on a process of class formation which would lead in the long run to a revolutionary overthrow of existing conditions.

Large-scale industry concentrates in one place a crowd of people unknown to one another. Competition divides their interests. But the maintenance of wages, this common interest which they have against their boss, unites them in a common thought of resistance-combination. Thus combination always has a double aim, that of stopping the competition among themselves, in order to bring about a general competition with the capitalist. If the first aim of the general resistance was merely the maintenance of wages, combinations, at first isolated, constitute themselves into groups as the capitalists in their turn united in the idea of repression, and in the face of always united capital, the maintenance of the association becomes more necessary to them than that of wages. This is so true that the English economists are amazed to see the workers sacrifice a good part of their wages in favor of associations, which in the eyes of the economists are established solely in favor of wages. In this struggle—a veritable civil war—are united and developed all the elements necessary for the coming battle. Once it has reached this point association takes on a political character.

Economic conditions had first transformed the mass of the people of the country into workers. The domination of capital has created for this mass a common situation, common interests. This mass is thus already a class as against capital, but not yet for itself. In this struggle, of which we have noted only a few phases, this mass becomes united, and constitutes itself as a class for itself. The interests it defends become class interests. But the struggle of class against class is a political struggle.[5]

In observing the beginnings of the modern labor movement, Mill and Marx came to different conclusions because they started from different premises. For Mill participation in government was the aim; for Marx it was the overthrow of capitalism. One made the workers' desire for social and political recognition the pivot of his interpretation, the other the desire to overcome the alienation of the work process. In the mid-nineteenth century, this difference of opinion was a matter of philosophical speculation mixed with observations of the English labor movement of the day. Today we can look back upon historical experience and—with all due caution—profit from the advantages of a retrospective judgment. We can put the speculations and observations of that earlier day into an abstract and also a comparative historical context.

To do this, we can start with the general experience of alienation which arose during the early phase of industrialization, but which appeared in the most diverse guises and elicited very different reactions.[6] The term "alienation" tacitly presupposes a feeling of "being-at-home," and the meaning of the concept changes with every modification of that sentiment. Mill's analysis refers to workers who wanted to participate in English national affairs. Even Engels conceded this point, though presumably without intending to do so. In a letter to Marx he wrote that "the English proletariat actually becomes ever more bourgeois so that this most bourgeois of nations finally seems intent upon possessing a bourgeois aristocracy and a bourgeois proletariat as well as a bourgeoisie."[7] At the time, England was the center of a world empire, and this setting made it plausible indeed for workers to lay claim to a larger portion of the country's prosperity. The struggle for the franchise and the demand for participation in government were expressions of that claim.

From this vantage point one can look at the situation in nineteenth-century Russia. Does it make sense to regard the recently recruited industrial work force of that country with assumptions similar to those made by Mill? The answer is "probably not." In tsarist Russia the emancipation of the serfs in 1861 helped to accelerate economic growth during the last decades of the century. But the emancipation was halfhearted, and its great burdens coincided with the exploitation and unintended brutalities of early Russian industrialization. It also coincided with the increasingly radical protest against tsarist rule which was largely the work of aristocrats and middle-class students and which culminated in the assassination of Tsar Alexander II in 1881. During the following years that protest also reached the ranks of the working class—as did the repressive measures of the government, for example, the double-edged weapon of police socialism (the so-called Zubatovchina), by which through a combination of threats and indoctrination the police coopted worker-activists who then would organize trade unions under police supervision. Even so, organizational experience and ideas of social justice spread among the workers. Workers certainly developed initiatives of their own; but the driving force of social protest consisted of revolutionaries from among the youths of the middle and upper strata of society. There were no developments of this second type in England.[8]

The impulse behind this movement of radical youth has been

formulated quite accurately by Peter Lavrov, an early participant and later exile.

> Every comfort which I enjoy, every thought which I had the leisure to acquire or work out, was purchased by blood, by the suffering of or by the labor of millions. I cannot correct the past, and no matter how dearly my development cost, I cannot renounce it. . . . Only the weak and intellectually backward person falters from the responsibility weighing upon him. . . . Evil has to be righted, insofar as that is possible, and it has to be done only during one's lifetime. . . . I remove from myself responsibility for the bloody cost of my development if I use this very development in order to lessen evil in the present and in the future. If I am a developed man, then I am obliged to do this.[9]

Privileged youths had a guilty conscience, and their sense of having to redeem their undeserved advantages by some sacrificial action was an important factor in the prehistory of the Russian Revolution. By contrast, one can hardly speak in this case of workers claiming a greater share in the prosperity of the country, for Russia was poor and her economic development uncertain. Any attempt to reconstruct the motivation of the Russian labor movement must take into account that the great turning points of its development—the emancipation of the serfs in 1861 and the two revolutions of 1905 and 1917—were repercussions of military defeat (in the Crimean War, the Russo-Japanese War, and World War I, respectively). Lost wars were also decisive in forming the attitudes and ideologies of the ruling strata of Russia. For a government which prides itself on military prestige, defeat in war is arguably the worst possible basis for extending the rights of citizenship to the lower strata. Such extension was neither desirable nor even conceivable from the standpoint of the tsarist government. On the other hand, there is no reason to assume that Russian workers were any less patriotic than Russian employers, though workers had to suffer under the prevailing conditions, whereas employers could profit from them. On the basis of these considerations, I would propose the following hypothetical explanation for the radicalization of the Russian labor movement.

The tsarist regime was militaristic in appearance and in its claims. But—with the single exception of its victory over Napoleon in 1812—it was actually on the losing side of the wars in Europe and the Far East. Given this record and the prevailing poverty, Russian workers could hardly feel thoroughly "at home" in their own country. Their fatherland was not "a success." Still, these workers were Russians, they knew no other country. During the last decades of the nineteenth century, however, reports reached them from abroad about successful trade unions and about the idea of a socialist society of the future. What then could be more plausible than that their ranks were gradually permeated by ideas about a new order in Russia to be organized along socialist lines? Their present homeland gave them no hope of greater participation in a more prosperous country. Hence workers gifted with some imagination were only consistent when they began to demand a country prosperous enough so that they also could participate in it. Accordingly, alienation in Russia meant something other than in England, but I think that the underlying national motivation was the same in both cases.

Looked at in this way, the Marxian approach appears in a rather different light than it usually does. Marx had been influenced by Hegelian and romantic ideas about work when he used as the basis of his analysis the possibility of self-realization through labor. In his view, every case of exploitation and the whole specialization of modern technology became sources of self-alienation for the industrial worker. By the same token, all efforts at mutual aid, trade union organizations, electoral campaigns, and ultimately the proletarian revolution would be so many steps in overcoming the alienation imposed by capitalism. Marx was well aware that self-realization, in contrast to alienation, is an individualist ideal which, like competition, leads to conflicts of interest among workers. Collective organization depended, therefore, on coalitions which would assume a political character through their struggles against the coalitions of employers. The success of the political labor movement depended upon a solidarity which would overcome the conflicts of interest dividing the working class.

Marx believed that these collective organizations would become widespread above all through the experience of the class struggle, and only secondarily through the leading role of communists. He also attributed more importance to the constraints of the industrial way of life and to the continuous class struggle than to the intermittent class consciousness of the workers themselves. In *The Holy Family* he wrote that workers are forced to be what they are by circumstances which are more important for the time being than what they themselves think.[10] For Marx, this leads to a split between "proletarians and communists" which would be overcome only in the course of development extending into the future. As the *Communist Manifesto* declares:

> The Communists are distinguished from the other working-class parties by this only: 1) In the national struggles of the proletarians of the different countries, they point out and bring to the front the common interests of the entire proletariat, independently of all nationality. 2) In the various stages of development which the struggle of the working class against the bourgeoisie has to pass through, they always and everywhere represent the interests of the movement as a whole. The Communists, therefore, are on the one hand, practically, the most advanced and resolute section of the working-class parties of every country, that section which pushes forward all others; on the other hand, theoretically, they have over the great mass of the proletariat the advantage of clearly understanding the line of march, the conditions, and the ultimate general results of the proletarian movement.[11]

Later on, the *Manifesto* states that the "workers have no fatherland," that they can become the leading class of the nation only through acquiring political domination. Yet this projection overestimates the international while underestimating the national ties of the industrial working class, a false assessment of nationalism rather than merely an unimportant mistake. Marx's error arose from the fact that he attributed world-historical importance to alienation in the work process and by implication to the ideal of self-realization. Neither alienation nor self-realization have that importance, however significant they may be as an individual experience. One can deplore the fact of nationalism. But we know today that "feeling at home" in one's own country ultimately means more to the people at large than the struggle for self-realization in or through the work process.

III

The contrast between the English and the Russian labor movement suggests that we should treat the English model with great caution. Industrialization can start only once. After that, previous experience influences later efforts. No other country which has begun to industrialize since the 1760s can start where England did. England is, therefore, the exception rather than the model—in contrast to the view expressed by Marx in his preface to *Capital,* that "the country that is more developed industrially only shows, to the less developed, the image of its own future."[12] True, for a time England possessed almost a monopoly of the most advanced techniques of production, and other countries copied these techniques through industrial espionage or through the employment of English craftsmen and technicians. During the first half of the nineteenth century England also took the lead by combining industrial with political superiority. One can understand in retrospect that as a result of these conditions, England developed a civic community in which the rising "fourth estate" finally managed to participate through a redefinition of rights and obligations. This singular case is important because it makes evident what other countries lacked, and particularly why the extension of citizenship to the lower strata is beset with difficulties. Even in England that extension was difficult enough.

In comparing industrial latecomers with England and democratic latecomers with France, the following question can be posed. What happens when a country lacks a "social contract" that can be said to function more or less adequately? Such functioning is always proximate. Nevertheless, we should distinguish a functioning political structure from one so backward that a country must first develop its institutional framework before the demand for citizenship makes much sense. The idea is hardly new that the protest of the lower classes can develop from a demand for citizenship in the existing political structure to a demand for a change of that structure. This idea is compatible with Marx's theory of progress from the machine breaking of the Luddites to a politically conscious labor movement. But the alienation of the people from an implicit social contract must be emphasized, not the alienation which arises from the lack of self-realization in the work process. This change of perspective makes it possible to see the connection between two mass movements of the nineteenth century which Marx saw as separate and in conflict with each other. For in his explanation of the socialist labor movement he assumed that nationalism would wither away as the class struggle became more intense. But socialist and nationalist agitation were in fact closely connected, insofar as both sought in different ways to achieve the extension of citizenship to all the people in order to overcome their social and political exclusion. This close connection was obscured, partly because Marx separated the two movements and partly because England's preeminence as a world power made it superfluous for her lower strata to demand a civic community to which they could be proud to belong.[13]

The perspective suggested here is not a mere reversal of Marx's theory. Marx sees the social movements of the nineteenth century as protests against psychic and material exploitation which would be transformed into political consciousness through an ever-mounting class struggle. Such transformation is indeed necessary if one assumes, as he does, that the desire for self-realization through work is the decisive motivation. That desire represents an important value, but I do not think it is an overriding historical factor. Instead, the protest movements of the nineteenth century were political from the start. They were different responses to the loss of social position—by people who were poor but proud, who wanted to regain that position under other conditions and in other forms.

From this vantage point, the eighteenth century appears as a turning point in the development of the lower strata in West European history. Before that time the mass of people could not claim public rights; since that time the people have gradually achieved citizenship, and to that extent they participate in an unwritten social contract. The Age of the Democratic Revolution (R. R. Palmer) extends from the eighteenth century to the present. During this period some countries have succeeded in the general extension of citizenship by peaceful means; others have not. Countries in the first group have managed to create a new, unwritten social contract, but only after having resolved major social upheavals. Still other countries have not found a solution to the problem and have become the victims of repeated coups d'état without tangible prospects of institutional stabilization. In a modern nation-state, the political problem of the lower strata is the process through which a national reciprocity of rights and duties is gradually enlarged and redefined. True, that process has been affected at every turn by forces emanating from the social and economic structure. The class struggle arising from the world of work is one such force, an important one but nevertheless only one of many. The alienation arising from the work process is not, I think, as decisive—even in the long run—as the distribution and redistribution of rights and obligations. The politics of distribution depend in large measure on the prosperity and international position of the country, upon shifting opinions concerning "just distribution" under these conditions, and upon the to and fro of the political struggle.[14] That distribution is not a mere by-product of the social structure.

My thesis goes hand in hand with Tocqueville's characterization of the political order as a reciprocity of rights and obligations. In nineteenth-century Europe, the growing consciousness of the working class was primarily expressed in a feeling of political alienation, the feeling that workers lacked a recognized place in bourgeois society or that there was no civic community in which a worker as such could participate. Legitimate political participation of the lower strata had become possible in European history for the first time. Hence protest of the lower strata against the social order was based at least initially on generally accepted rules of conduct, and it reflects a conservative state of mind even where it leads to violence against persons and property.[15] Instead of engaging in a chiliastic search for a new community, the newly politicized masses protest against the second-class citizenship imposed on them and insist on their right to participate as equal partners in the unwritten social contract of their country.[16] If this is a correct interpretation of the impulses and half-articulated wishes behind popular unrest in Western Europe, then we have a clue to the declining importance of socialism since the nineteenth century. The civic position of the lower strata is no longer an extraordinary problem in countries in which all strata of the population are accorded the rights of citizenship. But the fact is that new groups not previously considered part of the lower strata make claims to citizenship after the claims of older groups have become more or less satisfied. The problems of monopolization are not confined to the upper strata of society.

IV

In my analysis of this problem some twenty years ago, I assumed that citizenship for the lower strata in the industrialized countries of the West was a question of time. Accordingly, I entitled that part of my work "The extension of citizenship to the lower classes," a reference to T. H. Marshall's study distinguishing between civic, political, and social rights which was based on the English development. He showed that the lower strata had first to fight for civic equality, specifically for the right to form coalitions (a right which had been outlawed in 1799 but was restored in 1824, at least formally). The history of the franchise is more complex. But it is sufficient to state that in the course of the nineteenth century the right to vote was gradually freed of such earlier qualifications as property ownership or tax assessments of a certain amount. Also, the minimum voting age was lowered, and as a result the franchise was extended to ever larger segments of the working population. Social rights, the third element of citizenship in Marshall's terms, refer to health, unemployment, and disability insurance, as well as to the financing of schools and colleges out of public funds. All these welfare measures have the purpose of keeping the poverty of weaker strata of society within bounds while enlarging the chances of upward mobility of poor children by making school attendance compulsory. When I applied this model comparatively, it became apparent that each country had undergone its separate development, although all Western industrial societies had experienced a similar extension of citizenship. The details of these changes have since become the subject of an extensive literature.

But the industrialized societies of the West have witnessed structural changes since World War II, which raise doubts concerning the assumption that all workers and employees should and can enjoy an equality of citizenship. This assumption does not apply to most foreign workers, who have always been a part of the industrial work force. One report for Switzerland puts their proportion at 17 percent even as early as World War I, and the seasonal migration of Polish farmworkers into the German provinces east of the Elbe River was a common practice in the late nineteenth century. But within Western Europe as a whole, the influx of foreign workers has become a mass phenomenon only since World War II, so that today one is justified in speaking of a second proletariat in the industrialized countries of the West. There are, for example, Pakistanis, West Indians, and Indians from Africa in England; Algerians and Moroccans in France; Turks, Greeks, and Italians in West Germany; Yugoslavs in Sweden; and Mexicans and Puerto Ricans in the United States.

In the United States, with its population of 215 million people (1975–1977), some 105 million were (nonfarm) wage and salary earners in 1978; and of these, 24.6 million, or 23.4 percent, were organized in trade unions. On the other hand, in 1979 almost 11 million workers, or some 10 percent of the labor force, were black or Spanish-speaking minority groups which remained largely unorganized and held the lowest-paying jobs or were unemployed. In West Germany, the corresponding figures are 61.4 million total population (1976) and 26.8 million nonfarm wage and salary employees (1975), of whom 7.5 million (28 percent) were organized. In that year, a little over 10 percent of the work force in Germany consisted of foreigners. One can, therefore, speak of a large work force in these two nations; of a minority (about one-quarter) who are organized in trade unions; of a majority (about three-quarters) who are not organized; and, finally, of another minority, the "second proletariat," which earns the lowest wages, holds the worst jobs, and carries the burdens of discrimination. Similar conditions exist in other industrialized countries.

Thus, toward the end of the twentieth century, the industrialized West is confronted with the question whether and how this second proletariat, which meanwhile has become a permanent part of the social structure, can also be integrated into the political order. This is only in part a problem of citizenship, for some segments of this second proletariat are citizens already: for example, blacks in the United States or Commonwealth immigrants in England. In these cases citizenship as such does not mean much integration. Another segment does not want citizenship because they want to return to their homeland, though this return is delayed in many cases and its prospect gradually diminishes. Still others are illegal immigrants whose citizenship status is controversial. Such controversy is often inseparable from the position of the family, because foreign workers often become recipients of public assistance even while they remain foreigners. This can produce paradoxical situations, as in Germany, where Turkish parents have German-speaking children, but parents and children remain Muslims and do not really fit into a German community in linguistic, cultural, or religious terms.

And beyond all this: how do the trade unions deal with these foreign workers, if they take cognizance of them at all? What steps do schools, welfare agencies, and churches take in order to do justice to the concerns of these foreign migrants? Or does one leave such questions to the migrants themselves, insofar as they are willing and able to take the initiative? Or does this problem of internal integration finally become the object of international negotiations on the part of the home country, which may see in these migrants a loss of personnel if they have skills and a direct financial gain through remittances received from abroad, as well as a permanent issue in its relations with the host country?

The answers to these questions lie in the future. The closing years of the twentieth century bring with them problems pertaining to the citizenship of the lower strata which lie well outside the previous scope of the nation-state. Social scientists will find, I believe, that these problems have a prehistory in the intellectual mobilization which in the past has occurred in relatively backward countries in comparison with the technically and economically advanced parts of the world.

Six
Relative Backwardness and Intellectual Mobilization

Worldwide intellectual mobilization has accompanied and promoted the rise of the modern world. Intellectual mobilization has furthered the rise of nationalism and of the nation-state, and it has aided the transition from kings to people as the source of sovereignty. It is both a cause and a consequence of industrialization.

The comparative sketch of the situation around 1700 in Chapter 3 showed a world in which public affairs were confined to the privileged; society had a hierarchic rank order, and the mass of the people obeyed. Inequality was all-pervasive; the old regime was special only in the sense that its inequality was fixed legally as well as symbolically. Into this bastion of aristocratic privilege and lower-class subservience, notions of equality insinuated themselves gradually as land, labor, and capital, together with offices of government, became separated from considerations of family, inheritance, and social rank. True, ideas of equality had had their antecedents in the autonomous jurisdiction of medieval towns (roughly from the twelfth century on), in the leveling effect of firearms and of printing, in the Protestant idea of a "brotherhood of all believers," and in the individualizing notion of salvation by faith alone. But all these intimations of equality did nothing to alter the entrenched and well-articulated patriarchal relations between masters and servants until the commercialization of land, labor, and capital was well advanced and considerations of family and social rank had been superseded by market competition.

Then, the relations between the few and the many—and specifically the relations of employers and workers—were transformed in two ways. Within the enterprise, relations based on contract replaced those of status, and the sense of personal obligation diminished or disappeared. In the nation as a whole, rich and poor, employers and workers were now equal citizens under the law, which made the actual, glaring inequality between them all the more grating. I have described how new relations of command and obedience in the private sphere and an extension of citizenship in the public sphere were established. But these changes date from the late eighteenth century, that is, from the emergence of English industrial society, and they developed in other countries subsequently.

Intellectual mobilization and a national awakening are older processes than industrialization. They have spread throughout the world since the sixteenth century. Sooner or later they have been combined with the idea of government in the name of the people, regardless of what form governments of this nominal type have assumed. In today's world, neither monarchies nor military dictatorships hesitate to disguise their autocratic rule by populist justifications.

Intellectual mobilization—the growth of a reading public, of an educated secular elite dependent on learned occupations and related developments—has been a major cause of modernization in the two senses of popular sovereignty and industrialization. Recognition of intellectual mobilization as a cause of social change need not detract attention from such familiar processes associated with economic development and national citizenship as urbanization, the extension of the franchise, and the commercialization of land, labor, and capital. But there are movements since 1500—for example, the Reformation, and agitation for ethnic and religious autonomy, for freedom and equality—which do not have a *simple* basis in the division of labor or in class interest. Nationalism, which is among these complex movements, is noteworthy for the protean reaction to the international position of one's country which it causes across class lines. Ideas travel fast. In states that become aware of their backwardness in comparison with a more advanced nation, the search for ways to overcome that backwardness in the economic and political sense, and the effort to acquire a respected place among nations often precede every other kind of change. In the following discussion, intellectual mobilization will be considered first, then "demonstration effects" will be analyzed as a process of change that crosses national boundaries; in conclusion, the conflict will be treated between "modernizers" and "nativists" who want to advance their country, yet fear that the means used will jeopardize its cultural identity.

I

Since the sixteenth century, the world has been in permanent revolution, if by that phrase we understand the thoroughgoing, if often unwitting, transformation of social conditions due to technical and economic change, wars, political intervention, and outright revolution. In his *Novum Organum* (1620), Francis Bacon noted that printing, gunpowder, and the magnet had "changed the whole face and state of things throughout the world."[1] Guns mounted on ships were the technical means by which explorers and conquerors initiated the age of European expansion overseas.[2] The lifetimes of the great explorers (Columbus, 1446?–1506; da Gama, 1469?–1524; Magellan, 1480?–1521) overlapped with those of Luther (1483-1546) and Copernicus (1473-1543) so that there is a broad concurrence between exploration, overseas expansion, and the transformation of the prevailing religious and scientific world-views. All of this had been preceded by the invention of printing; the first Gutenberg Bible appeared sometime before 1456. The number of educated people increased, as did the number of those whose livelihood depended upon teaching, writing, or some other intellectual vocation. The new facility of printing explains why overseas exploration, the Reformation, and the early development of science resulted in a burgeoning literature of travelogues, religious pamphlets, and scientific and political tracts.[3] I call this whole process of a more rapid reproduction and diffusion of ideas, and the related increase in the number of writers and readers, "intellectual mobilization."

Facilitated by the invention of printing, old learned occupations turned secular, new professions based on learning developed, governments became bureaucratic, and secular education rose to social esteem and functional importance.[4] Furthermore, the Reformation gave impetus to literacy among the middle and lower strata of the population, and, later, writing became an independent, secular profession.[5] In the course of these transformations, many people became consumers of secular culture, whereas formerly they had been confined to religious observances and popular amusements. This emergence of a culture-consuming public is the background for the intellectual leadership of an active minority of lawyers, teachers, ministers, writers, and many others.

There is a correlation between economic backwardness and intellectual mobilization, and it was described by the German folklorist Wilhelm Riehl in the late 1840s. In a chapter entitled "The Intellectual Proletariat," Riehl wrote that this group

> represents the great vanguard of that social stratum which has broken with the traditional social structure, openly and self-consciously. . . .
>
> I think of this group of the fourth estate in the broadest terms. It consists of a proletariat of civil servants, a proletariat of schoolmasters, perennial students of theology, starving academic instructors, literati, journalists, artists of all kinds ranging downwards from the travelling virtuosi to the itinerant comedians, organ-grinders and vaudeville singers. . . . In Germany, the turnover of the nation's material capital is disproportionately small compared with this wholesale and retail trade, this hawking and profiteering in spiritual goods. Germany produces more mental product than she can use or pay for. . . .
>
> We are confronted with a vicious circle. Intellectual work shoots up like weeds, because economic enterprise does not provide it with sufficiently extensive opportunities for growth, and this growth in turn cannot come to fruition, because every surplus of energy is dissipated in an endless foliage of books.[6]

Riehl had genuine insight into the uneven pace of the intellectual, economic, and social development of a country, and that insight applies quite generally to follower societies of the nineteenth and twentieth centuries. But Riehl's conservatism put him out of sympathy with the intellectuals he described, and he failed to see that their mobilization was a general attribute of European countries that were developing a national identity.

In late sixteenth-century England, three groups developed which eventually coalesced in opposition to the rule of Charles I. The first group consisted of Puritan divines, led by men who had been persecuted under the reign of Mary Tudor. After Elizabeth came to the throne in 1558, these men hoped to purify the Anglican church of its Catholic legacies in doctrine and ritual, but they intended to do so from within the church through reform of the church service, the presbyterian principle of organization, and widespread lecturing.[7] The second group consisted of lawyers, members of a conservative profession, many of whom had a guildlike interest in the common-law courts as against the prerogative courts of the king.[8] The third group consisted of prominent landed gentry in Parliament, men of great standing in the realm who sponsored the Puritan clergy through their control of church benefices and employed lawyers in their many lawsuits. These aristocratic representatives of "the country" were often legally trained, and many were themselves Puritans.[9] The ties of interest which linked these three groups have been the subject of much controversy. But there is less dispute that these men of faith, vested interest, and high social standing were originally prompted by the English Reformation to define the position and aspirations of their country in conscious opposition to the Spanish world empire and its alliance with the papacy in attacking the English heresy.[10]

The development of eighteenth-century France can be described in analogous terms. Louis XIV died in 1715, leaving a country that was culturally and politically preeminent in the world but exhausted from the decades of war leading to that position.[11] In the wake of his reign, opposition to the ancien régime and ultimately to the monarchy showed a strong convergence of theoretical principles, vested interests, and high social standing. The philosophes formulated their doctrine of natural rights in opposition to church and nobility under the inspiration of Newton and Locke. The famous *Encyclopédie,* which began publication in 1751, linked a burgeoning natural science which found universal acclaim with the principles of reason and natural law applied to man and society. Soon these beliefs were taken up by others whose social position gave weight to their opinions. One group consisted of the *parlementaires,* the *noblesse de robe* who served the sovereign courts of France primarily in a judicial capacity. But these *parlementaires,* especially those of Paris, had the right and duty to register governmental edicts without which no royal decree was legally valid; and when they refused to do so, as they often did in the eighteenth century, they used the language of the philosophes to justify their actions. Another group consisted of the high French nobility, congregating not only at the Versailles court, but in the salons and Masonic lodges of Paris, where they mingled freely with the luminaries of French culture. Note that the language of the philosophes, the *parlementaires,* and the nobility was suffused with ideas derived from English parliamentary institutions and from the struggle for independence of the American colonies. Thus, opinions of the educated elite (which led up to the French Revolution) were mobilized by invidious comparisons between the freedoms achieved or fought for in England and America and the vested interests and abrogation of rights characteristic of the French ancien régime.[12]

The French revolution and the populist revolutions which followed must be distinguished from the English revolutions of 1640 and 1688. The mainstream of English revolutionary thought was limited by the religious and legal contexts in which the old justifications of authority had been questioned. English theory and practice remained compatible with the restoration of oligarchic rule, though on the new basis of the king-in-Parliament. By contrast, French revolutionary thought went beyond such limitations because it made the people and the nation the basis of all authority. Note also that in both cases the movement toward revolution was spearheaded by men of education and standing in the established society of their day.

As one observes old societies that have been on the periphery of Europe's outward thrust over the centuries, or as one moves east in Europe itself during the nineteenth century, one finds countries in which neither an educated elite nor representative institutions nor an economically and politically active bourgeoisie and aristocracy are indigenous developments, or at any rate not vigorous ones. Such countries are arenas of intellectual mobilization in which officials, teachers, literati, and other members of Riehl's "intellectual proletariat" tend to coalesce into a class of their own. That class consists of ideological groups which are sensitive to developments beyond their country's frontiers and anxious to find a more viable mode of social organization for their native land.

II

A revolution occurs when a social order is drastically transformed and reconstituted. Though revolutions are conventionally identified with lower-class movements, a "revolution from above" can be equally far-reaching. Indeed, restorations can prove as revolutionary as revolutions. The Meiji restoration of 1868 is a good example, for the Meiji government restructured the whole political and social order of Tokugawa Japan. Should this restructuring be called a revolution even though it was undertaken in the interest of national survival against Western incursions and it quickly entailed the imposition of new restraints? It should, because both nationalism and the reassertion of authority are found in many (possibly all) modern revolutions.

Modern history has been characterized by consecutive revolutions or restorations, and each of these transformations has influenced the next. In the sixteenth and seventeenth centuries, England began these great upheavals with the Henrician reformation, the civil war and revolution of 1640–1660, and the "glorious revolution" of 1688. These were followed by the industrial and the French revolutions of the eighteenth century, the Prussian reforms (1807–1814) and the unification of Germany under Bismarck (1870–1871), the Meiji restoration of Japan in 1868, and the transformation of Russia from the emancipation of the serfs in 1861 to the Bolshevik revolution of 1917 and the Stalinist revolution of 1928. Each of these revolutions or restorations was a collective response to both internal conditions *and* external stimuli. Each had repercussions beyond the frontiers of the country in which it occurred. After each transformation, the world changed in Heraclitus' sense that you cannot step into the same river twice. Once the English king had been overthrown and Parliament declared supreme, other monarchies became insecure and the idea of parliamentary government was launched. Once industrialization was initiated, other economies became backward. Once the idea of equality had been proclaimed before a worldwide audience, inequality became a burden too heavy to bear.[13]

Sixteenth-century England was still comparatively slow in creating a market for labor and capital, but the country witnessed a flourishing trade, a rapid increase in the sale and purchase of land (commercialization), and a high degree of intellectual mobilization. The awareness that England had become a nation promoted self-confidence, though this was mixed with apprehension. In relation to the Spanish world empire, Englishmen still thought of their country as a small island on the margins of a continent. Spain dominated the western Mediterranean and had colonized the globe; France dominated Europe; and the pope controlled an international church whose hierarchy extended to all civilized countries. The Spanish empire, France, and the Catholic church were the "reference societies" to which the intellectual leaders and the educated public of England responded emotionally and politically. The results of those responses can be termed "demonstration effects."[14]

Two centuries later, observers of the industrial revolution were impressed—and rightly so—by the role that the division of labor played in the economic development of all Western European societies. But the division of labor developed in one country can become the model followed by another. In the sixteenth century, Holland was the most advanced country commercially, and Dutch commercial and manufacturing processes were quickly emulated in England. A century later, the industrial revolution began in England, and other countries followed the English model when they began to develop their own industry. But then they wished to follow the *latest* English development to which they could gain access, not the English practices of the 1760s with which English industrialization had begun. Countries were therefore less and less able or willing to repeat the development of others. Nor were they likely to become the same kind of societies as a result of successful industrialization. Continued organizational and cultural differentiation were the more likely outcome. The demonstration effect prevented societies from repeating others' development and thus hindered industrial societies from converging culturally and institutionally.[15]

The French Revolution is a striking example of this point. During the prehistory of that revolution, Frenchmen responded variously to antecedent events abroad, ranging from English political institutions, the concepts of Newton and Locke, and the American war of independence to ideas derived from classical antiquity—and all this was combined with the problems bequeathed to France by Louis XIV. But once the French Revolution had occurred, other countries could not and did not recapitulate that prehistory; they reacted to the revolution itself instead. Thus, German rulers of the eighteenth and nineteenth centuries, in an effort to maintain their inherited authority, proposed to do for "their" people by a revolution from above what the French people had done from below at high cost by and for themselves.[16]

In the twentieth century, the Russian Revolution became—at least for a time—the reference society, whether positively or negatively. Russia's overthrow of an old regime in an economically backward society and its forced collectivization and industrialization were achieved at enormous cost. Under the leadership of Mao Tse-tung, the Chinese reacted to this model by accepting a slower rate of economic growth with a positive emphasis on the peasantry, on re-education campaigns, and on the importance of subjective commitment as a major cause of change. By linking these policies with the Chinese tradition they have created a new revolutionary model. Today, Communist China has its own demonstration effects on other countries.

These examples are diverse but all of them refer to an archetypical experience: there is always an educated minority or intelligentsia which sees its own country as backward in comparison with some advanced country. This is a troubled perception, for it identifies strength if not goodness with alien forces and sees weakness if not evil in one's homeland. In this setting, ideas are used to mobilize forces capable of effecting change and, one hopes, of redressing this psychologically unfavorable accounting.

Typical arguments follow which involve some measure of wishful thinking applied to real events. To the person in the backward country the strength of the advanced country appears formidable; but that strength is also perceived as sapped by false values, corruption, and spiritual decay, and "therefore" such a country should not and cannot endure. The same person may be aware that his native land is weak, but he searches for the hidden spiritual values of his people, which can be an untapped source of strength and perhaps will prevail in the end. Thus the dominance of the advanced country carries within it the seeds of its own destruction, whereas the backward people and the underdeveloped country possess capacities that are signs of a bright future. Behind this strategy of argument lies the simple belief that ultimately the advanced country must be weak because its culture and people are evil, but the backward country must be strong because its culture and people are good.

Such wishful thinking has been an important factor in nationalist efforts to achieve the social and economic development of backward countries by routes other than those followed by the pioneering country. But this archetype of intellectual mobilization under conditions of relative backwardness provides only a model. When sensitive and articulate men and women suffer from the weakness and deprivation that is all around them, they will leave no avenue untried to better the fortunes of their country and its people. When practical measures to do so are unavailable, free play is given to ideas. The result is a kaleidoscope of national aspirations linked to a world history of uneven development and worldwide inequalities.

Events in Iran between 1979 and 1982 are a case in point. The Iranians and, more generally, Muslim peoples of the Middle East have an intense wish for the American presence to disappear. Yet, at the same time, the strategic and economic importance of oil, the threat of Soviet invasion, and the Arab-Israeli conflict continuously reinforce Arab relations with the United States. In addition to these geopolitical factors, there are ideological reasons for the Muslim ambivalence toward the West. As Marvin Zonis has stated:

> Islam is in the minds of true believers a perfect religion. It is perfect in the sense that it represents completion. . . . Mohammed is the last prophet who ever was, or will be. He is the last prophet

who will bring divine revelation. There will be other great thinkers, but there will be none with divine revelation, a chain which began with Adam, Noah, Abraham, Moses, and Jesus and was sealed by *The* Prophet. In short, mankind has been delivered the complete message through The Prophet Mohammed.

In an interview I had with Ayatollah Khomeini, he assured me that the Islamic Republic of Iran would work because Islam, which is its guiding force, was "the complete faith." Islam embodied everything that the West has separated from religion: economics, politics, social relationships, and culture.

Not only is Islam complete, and, therefore, superior to all other religions, but Muslims have taken it upon themselves to spread the recognition of this fact. It is not enough for Muslims to recognize the superiority of their own faith; others must do so as well. Others must express a recognition of the completeness and perfection of Islam. One reason for the rather shrill insistence of Muslims that we pay attention to them and respect their religion is that our recognition undergirds their belief that their religion is complete and perfect.

The "abode of Islam" will reign powerfully, of course, only insofar as it maintains interaction with the West. The game is in the interaction. For the status of Islam is a relative one, determined by comparison with Europe and the United States. And note, the interaction, at least for the time being, takes the form of a "zero-sum" competition. There can only be one winner and the gains of the winner must be at the expense of the loser. . . .

The powerful desire to eliminate the long-standing sense of humiliation and the need for ideological support of Islam will lead, for the next decade, to further exacerbating, aggravating, and difficult interactions between the West and the Muslim world.[17]

Alexander Herzen once wrote that "human development is a form of chronological unfairness, since late-comers are able to profit by the labours of their predecessors without paying the same price."[18] He neglected to mention the unprecedented problems which new states face and the price they must pay for "human development." Indeed, the problems facing each modernizing country are largely unique. Even nations which have been building their political institutions for centuries still have to cope with the repercussions of their process of modernization. Today new states looking for analogies or precedents in other countries have more models to choose from than ever before, but their own histories and the earlier development of other countries do not prepare them for the tasks of nation building which lie ahead.

III

These tasks have been formidable throughout history but perhaps they are even more awesome in a twentieth-century setting. Demonstration effects make it impossible to repeat earlier developments; and the effort of learning from the developments of other countries is beset by difficulty and—pace Herzen—the price may be high. Every idea taken from elsewhere can be both an asset to the development of a country and a reminder of its comparative backwardness, that is, both a challenge to be emulated and, whatever its utility, a threat to national identity. What appears desirable from the standpoint of progress often appears dangerous to national independence. The revolution in communications since the fifteenth century has been accompanied by ever new confrontations with this cruel dilemma.

The contemporary world has made us familiar with the tension between progress and national identity. Each country must cope socially and politically with the disruptive impact of ideas and industrial practices taken from abroad. Its ability or inability to do so is conditioned to a considerable extent by its own history. The old societies which have recently become new states look back upon centuries of historical experience involving a mixture of languages, economic systems, and religious beliefs.[19] This is the base from which they must master the impact of the "advanced world." Only by understanding the peculiarities of each affected civilization can we begin to assess how different countries will cope, or fail to cope, with the ideas and institutions of the industrially and politically influential countries.

The advanced countries of today have had their own periods of underdevelopment and of responding to the "advanced world" of their day. They have grappled for centuries with internal divisions and with the problems of political integration, and they still struggle (as all countries must) with the unresolved legacies of their several histories. For example, "England" does not include

Scotland and Wales and is a misleading name for the United Kingdom of Great Britain and Northern Ireland. Scottish nationalism, Welsh language and culture, and the continuing struggles in Northern Ireland certainly reinforce that point.[20] Ethnic, linguistic, and religious divisions pose ever-changing problems of political accommodation, and societies are unified only in the sense that they have learned to handle such diversities. Terms like "state" or "nation" play down or ignore these persistent divisions, but political unity is never complete, and serious challenges to it recur to this day even in the old states.

In the new states, the predominance of civil ties over the affinities of language, religion, and ethnicity is a much more recent and precarious development. As noted earlier, fifty-one countries founded the United Nations in 1945; by 1976, ninety-one additional countries had been admitted to that body. Most new states have had to establish their governments on a new basis, defining "the people" as their ultimate source of authority. In the new states, nationalist appeals to legitimacy are heard frequently— even in the absence of war. In the old states, war has often been an important foundation of political culture and institutions.

Nationalism, however, though a nearly universal phenomenon in modern history, is not in fact a force that easily unifies countries. Indeed, the old states underwent long periods of intellectual polarization when they had to come to terms with challenges from abroad. The typical response—and it is evident today in the new states—is a polarization of modernizers and nativists. One example of this phenomenon is the debate in eighteenth- and nineteenth-century Japan between those who advocated national learning (*kokugaku*) and desired to derive all guidance from Japanese tradition, and those who advocated Dutch learning (*rangaku*) and desired to complement their native heritage with Western knowledge.[21] Another example is found in Russia, the gradual transformation of whose "backwardness" is indistinguishable from its responses to the West. The conflict between modernizers and traditionalists is evident in the debates of the Nikonian reformers and the Old Believers over the introduction of "foreign" ideas into the Orthodox church in the seventeenth century and in the debates of the Westernizers and Slavophiles in the nineteenth century.

The modernizers and nativists of a country share the desire to preserve and enhance their native land—as they share their hostility to the "advanced country." A Westernizer like Herzen comments on his "elective affinity" with the Slavophiles: "like Janus, or the two-headed eagle, we looked in opposite directions, but one heart beats in our breasts."[22] All the same, such groups are deeply divided over which path to modernization their country should follow.

In the examples of Englishmen responding to the dangers, as they saw it, represented by Spain and the Catholic church in the sixteenth century, or of Chinese to the dangers and the promise of "Mr. Science" and "Mr. Democracy" of the West in the early twentieth century, a pattern emerges. The perception of advances abroad is a reminder of backwardness or dangers and weakness at home. Intellectuals attempt to cope with the ensuing dilemma: Whether to adopt the advanced model and invite its attending corruptions, or fall back upon native traditions and risk their inappropriateness to the world of power and progress. This dilemma engenders heated debates and ever uneasy compromises which have their common denominator in a shared concern for the native country. Such intensive debates prompted by common concerns are a foundation of nationalism. The result need not be divisive: a traditionalist like Gandhi and a modernizer like Nehru could work together in their opposition to British rule. But the debates between traditionalists and modernizers remain unresolved more often than not, both during the struggle against an old regime and after it has been overthrown and a new regime established.

Before as well as after the revolution the root causes of that division remain. Men want their country recognized and respected in the world, and to this end they cultivate or revive native traditions. The reconstruction of history is an act of reconsecrating authority in the name of the people. It is an appeal to civic loyalty and national brotherhood in lieu of more divisive communal attachments, because birth in a common homeland makes all people members of one nation sharing equally in its past glories. But the desire to be recognized and respected in the world also calls for the development of a modern economy and a government which focuses attention upon one (or more than one) selected advanced society or societies. This reference to foreign models has become inescapable since the great intellectual mobilization of the sixteenth century.

In our world, the sense of backwardness in one's own country has led to ever new encounters with the advanced model or development of another country. Within the context of modern communications and uneven development, this process of historical models and their demonstration effects continues to the present, and I cannot see an end to its further ramifications.

Several countries have been in the world-historical position of providing demonstration effects. In the twentieth century, old models have been replaced once more. After Spain and Portugal, after England and France, it is now the turn of the United States, the USSR, and China to be the models. Any heir of the Western tradition will watch the new states with concern and empathy, for in their present form they are largely the result of Western expansion. It is the task of these new countries of the Third World to blend renewed traditions with the demands of modern development under the conditions of the twentieth century.

This prospect is one of great uncertainty which no research of the rationalistic type is capable of reducing significantly. The events of the late 1970s and early 1980s in Iran have resulted in many articles and books which deal persuasively with what went wrong in the late Shah's projects of forced modernization. There may be merit in these reflections. But they cannot come to grips with the fact that events of religious significance which occurred some thirteen hundred years ago are capable even today of creating a political firestorm which has spread to many Islamic countries and will affect their relations with the West for years and decades to come. True, the historicist approach would probably increase our uncertainty, because it is designed to alert us to the potential for change which exists in the background of all contemporary facts and developments, not just those of Islam. But this greater awareness of uncertainty is due to the legacies which history has bestowed on every country; and if we cultivate such awareness and move cautiously forward with the scientific and technical advances which are our fate, we can prepare ourselves psychologically for the future in which we and our children will live. And that is a worthy goal of education in the social sciences today.

Appendix: An Exchange
of Letters Between the Author
and a Graduate Student

Berkeley, California
April 19, 1982

Dear Professor Bendix,

I attended your recent lectures and enjoyed them. In the course of this series you successfully tamed my utopian tendencies, not to mention what totalitarian impulses might lurk in the darker recesses of the average soul. This viewpoint corresponds with my own reading of Weber, who similarly dispels "illusions" of objective purpose and warns of the excesses of "absolutist" ethics.

Yet there is another side to Weber that I do not think was given sufficient voice in your presentation, namely that secular Protestantism that stands up and declares, "Here I stand, I can do no other." What of the actor, political or scholarly, who is well aware that the historical consequences of his actions cannot correspond sufficiently with his initial intentions, but who acts "In spite of all!" even in the face of that knowledge.

Merleau-Ponty once wrote that Weber's social scientific activity could best be understood as a desperate attempt to hold together in his person a world that was about to fly apart. It is this daemonic commitment, this Faustian affirmation of his own inner-worldly activity, that gives integrity and meaning to Weber's vocation as a scholar and activist.

You stated that knowledge is linked to purposes. You suggested throughout that modern science is something like the latest response to the questions of *theodicy,* of coping intellectually with irrationalities and with the place of privilege and misfortune in the world. You further suggested that the North-South issue of economic backwardness is an example of these problems.

My question is what you perceive to be that purpose of social science in the present epoch, in this post-Weberian world in which it is not at all clear that we in the North bear a moral relationship to our neighbors in the South, a relationship which, if moral and binding, is not only to be known and coped with intellectually but must be acted upon. It is Weber's passionate sense of responsibility (evident in his last two lectures on politics and science as vocation) that I found absent from your very even-handed and balanced approach to the "big" issues of history and society.

With regards,

John Seery
*[Graduate student,
Department of Political Science,
University of California, Berkeley]*

Berkeley, California
April 26, 1982

Dear John Seery:

Your thoughtful letter of April 19 deserves a careful response, even though neither you nor I may be satisfied with it. Then, also, no one else may have an adequate answer, but let me give it a try.

Weber's alternative between an ethic of conviction and an ethic of responsibility may be an ultimate one, there may be no way of bridging the two. I am not sure that this is so, but if it is, then there cannot be an answer to that ethical dilemma in our proximate human world. Put another way: the alternative between conviction and responsibility is an ideal typical one which is removed from our daily experience. In actuality, our lives consist of admixtures, and the conceptual distinctions we make disentangle these admixtures and remove the discussion from our daily experience.

I share Weber's commitment to an ethic of responsibility, particularly in the one field in which I *am* acting, namely the pursuit of knowledge. It is often undertaken without a sense of purpose, but I believe strongly that it should not be. My effort was to show that the conviction "knowledge equals progress" (the rationalistic approach) is unwarranted in this bald form, because it promises more than it can fulfill. That was my reason for exploring the implications of an "historicist" approach with its diminished expectations and claims. Of course, historicism has purposes of its own, but you are right that I was not explicit in stating these purposes. I was preoccupied instead, as you realize, with exemplifying the substantive meaning of the historicist approach, as I have tried to develop it in my work.

In my view, modern science including social science is *not* the latest response to the questions of theodicy, as your letter suggests. The whole record of the history of science is against that interpretation. At its beginning, Francis Bacon openly broke with that theological tradition by advocating practical in addition to speculative reason. However, it is quite true that the believers in "knowledge equals progress" have frequently made it sound as if this formula was tantamount to a secular theodicy, which is a contradiction, blasphemous in religious terms, and quite unrealistic in secular terms as well. I hold instead that the pursuit of knowledge can (but need not) improve the human condition, and even when it does, it also creates problems for those who benefit from that increased knowledge. The question is whether the benefits of increased knowledge outweigh the problems created.

Which brings me to your question of the purposes of social science in the present epoch. At one level, they are not different from the purposes of knowing more about man and nature than we do now. That is the ultimate commitment for knowledge and against ignorance without which no pursuit of knowledge makes sense. You might call it our fortune and misfortune, for it is part of the historical legacy which our forebears fashioned consciously, and from which we can extricate ourselves only by resorting to religious or quasi-religious answers. No one who makes use of the results of modern knowledge in his daily life can live consistently without acknowledging this commitment. (As a beneficiary of open-heart surgery, I owe my life to this commitment.)

But this commitment is no longer as untroubled as it was even a generation ago. You know all the reasons from atomic bombs and the disposal of nuclear waste to the unanticipated side effects of most innovations. In a perverse way, we can be grateful that the social sciences are less effective than the natural sciences: we do less harm and we do less good.

Do we do any good? Potentially, I believe we do. I wrote about this thirty years ago, though I see more clearly now what I saw then. Allow me the indulgence of quoting myself: "It is quite legitimate to conduct social science research projects which are useful in the short run. But it is both illegitimate and unwise to make claims for their long-run utility, especially since these claims are no longer sustained by a faith in progress or in the Divine order of things. . . . In the long run it would be far more *useful* to take our stand on the ground that our intellectual life is enriched by worthwhile research in the social sciences. Such research is [today I would say "can be"] a token of high civilization, as an integral part of our quest for knowledge. This quest manifests our abiding faith in the constructive and enriching *possibilities* of human reason. This is not a disinterested statement. In a world torn by wars of nerves, arms, and words the universities ought to be institutions of detachment, whose academic personnel have an important service to render in the community, for which they should claim recognition from the powers that be. It is the task of the social sciences to further the work of human enlightenment, not to claim a utility which they frequently lack. Social scientists should have an abiding faith in human reason, even if they are often without the old religious foundations of such a faith. This is a more humane creed than a concern with improving the techniques of social manipulation. It is the only position worthy of the great intellectual traditions in which they stand. It is the baseline of the intellectual defense against the threat of totalitarianism."

Today I would add only that the major purpose of the social sciences is educational, the never-ending effort to achieve improvements in the quality of judgment; that by its nature this goal is long-run; and that long-run "utilities" like this are at a discount in a pragmatic world. That does not make them less worthy of our earnest effort. But we can attain this goal only so long as we are honest about the purposes of advancing knowledge and about the kind of knowledge we seek.

These are the reasons why I feel that the "big issues" of history and society are not absent from my approach, but certainly my expectations are modest and long-run. That is probably the reason why I appear less torn and passionate than Weber was, and no doubt less "great" (with or without quotation marks). Trying to hold the world together by containing its tensions within one person seems to me a futile endeavor for a secular man. In this sense Weber was religious despite his denials, seeking secular answers for dilemmas of the human condition which each of the world religions, as he shows so well, has resolved in its own way. For myself, I think it futile to seek secular answers to the ultimate questions of human existence, such as the meaning of life or of history. It is difficult to be content with this position at any age, but I think Weber shows us that it is as hard, or harder, to attempt secular answers to religious dilemmas in an age of disbelief.

With best personal regards and special thanks for your thoughtful letter.

Cordially,
Reinhard Bendix

Notes

FOREWORD

1. Max Weber, *The Methodology of the Social Sciences,* trans. and ed. Edward Shils and Henry Finch (Glencoe:Free Press, 1949), p. 72.
2. See *ibid.,* p. 74; and "Author's Introduction" in Max Weber, *The Protestant Ethic and the Spirit of Capitalism,* trans. Talcott Parsons (New York: Charles Scribner's Sons, 1958), pp. 13ff.
3. On this point see also Guenther Roth, "Introduction to the New Edition," in Reinhard Bendix, *Max Weber: An Intellectual Portrait* (Berkeley: University of California Press, 1977), pp. xvff.
4. Reinhard Bendix, "Geistige Existenz und fragwürdige Gruppenzugehörigkeit," in *Mannheimer Berichte* (October, 1980), p. 60.

CHAPTER I

1. See Hans Barth, *Truth and Ideology,* trans. Frederic Lilge (Berkeley: University of California Press, 1976).

2. Michael Todaro, *Economic Development in the Third World* (London: Longman, 1977), p. 94.
3. See W. W. Rostow, *The Stages of Economic Growth: A Non-Communist Manifesto* (London: Cambridge University Press, 1960).
4. Guy E. Swanson, "Frameworks for Comparative Research: Structural Anthropology and the Theory of Action," in *Comparative Methods in Sociology,* ed. Ivan Vallier (Berkeley, University of California Press, 1971), p. 145.
5. Neil J. Smelser, *Comparative Methods in the Social Sciences* (Englewood Cliffs, N.J.: Prentice-Hall, 1976), p. 154.
6. Francis Bacon, "Novum Organum," in *The English Philosophers from Bacon to Mill,* ed. E. A. Burtt (New York: Modern Library, 1939), p. 29.
7. This immersion of the scholar and his subject in the historical process is an insight of Max Weber. Karl Löwith writes: "This fact alone, that Weber includes his own scientific propensity in the historical peculiarity and problematic character of our entire modern life, distinguishes him fundamentally from the scientific zeal which is entirely specialized and unaware of its own presuppositions, and also from the naive faith in science professed by most Marxists. . . . Scientific research depends upon implicit presuppositions of the human condition of the most decisive and detailed significance, because man is the precondition of the specialist. For this very reason Weber insists on a task that is not a matter of specialized sociology but of social philosophy, namely to make explicit in each case the 'a priori' of the guiding values *within* each specific research project. Such inquiry into values must appear inevitably sterile to the specialist, for indeed—as Weber himself occasionally emphasized—nothing comes of it, i.e., a nothing in the sense of positive scientific progress. Still, what does result is a philosophical contribution to an understanding of the possible meaning of scientific objectivity and knowledge." See Karl Löwith, *Gesammelte Abhandlungen* (Stuttgart: W. Kohlhammer, 1960), pp. 9–10, 12. It should be added that in recent decades both the development of modern physics and of the philosophy of science have

raised questions concerning the effect on his observations of nature of the scientist's position in nature.

8. My formulation is modeled after an idea of Zygmunt Bauman, *Hermeneutics and Social Science* (London: Hutchinson, 1978), pp. 44–47. But because I deviate from Bauman on some decisive points, I emphasize my own formulation.

9. See Reinhard Bendix, "Science and the Purposes of Knowledge," *Social Research* 46 (Winter 1975), 331–359. See also my formulation of this position in 1951, which was the starting point of my comparative research, in *Social Science and the Distrust of Reason,* University of California Publications in Sociology and Social Institutions (Berkeley: University of California Press, 1951).

10. Jacob Burckhardt, *Force and Freedom: Reflections on History* (New York: Pantheon, 1943), p. 90. Whereas Burckhardt addresses himself to the "purpose of knowledge," Karl Popper has made the related logical point that science and technology are among the determinants of the future, and to presume to know the effects of future inventions in these fields is tantamount to anticipating those inventions. A future anticipated in the present is no longer a future. See Karl Popper, *The Poverty of Historicism* (London: Longman, 1961). There are other determinants of the future than progress-oriented science and technology—nor do these determinants depend on prediction, as science and technology do. Burckhardt's generic point applies to art and religion, e.g., whereas Popper's logical point does not.

11. Daniel Lerner, *The Passing of Traditional Society,* 2nd ed. (Glencoe: Free Press, 1964), p. 46.

12. *Ibid.,* pp. 65–68.

13. David Riesman, "Introduction," in *ibid.,* p. 10.

14. Clark Kerr et al., *Industrialism and Industrial Man* (Cambridge: Harvard University Press, 1960), pp. 33ff.

15. *Ibid.,* pp. 19f., 47ff.

16. *Ibid.,* p. 49.

17. Alex Inkeles and David H. Smith, *Becoming Modern* (London: Heinemann, 1974), pp. 8–14.

18. Gabriel Almond and James Coleman, *The Politics of the*

Developing Areas (Princeton: Princeton University Press, 1960), p. 4.

19. Fernand Braudel, *The Mediterranean and the Mediterranean World in the Age of Philip II*, 2 vols. (New York: Harper & Row, Harper Torchbooks, 1975), II, p. 1244.

20. Fernand Braudel, *Afterthoughts on Material Civilization and Capitalism* (Baltimore: Johns Hopkins University Press, 1977), p. 3. See also the discussion by Guenther Roth, "Duration and Rationalization: Braudel and Weber," in Guenther Roth and Wolfgang Schluchter, *Max Weber's Vision of History* (Berkeley: University of California Press, 1979), pp. 166–194.

21. These comments are based on conversations with Fernand Braudel during our stay as colleagues at the Woodrow Wilson International Center for Scholars, Smithsonian Institution, Washington, D.C., during the academic year 1975–76. Braudel described how he had written the largest part of his Mediterranean text in Mainz as a German prisoner of war, and how after his return to Paris he and his wife had spent months in the basement of their house, adding to the text the many hundreds of footnotes he had collected in many European archives in the years before the war.

22. Immanuel Wallerstein, *The Capitalist World-Economy* (New York: Cambridge University Press, 1979), pp. x–xii.

23. This threefold distinction is most briefly described in *ibid.*, pp. 155ff.

24. Immanuel Wallerstein, *The Modern World-System, Capitalist Agriculture and the Origins of the European World-Economy in the Sixteenth Century*, 2 vols. to date (New York: Academic Press, 1974), I, 347.

25. *Ibid.* In this quotation I have omitted the organismic analogy which the author applies to the world system because this analogy leads to problems which are irrelevant to this discussion.

26. The statement in quotation marks and the reference to astronomy are in *ibid.*, pp. 7, 348. My paraphrasing is based on the author's own words.

27. Wallerstein, *Capitalist World-Economy*, pp. vii–xii.

28. *Ibid.*, p. 164.

29. *Ibid.*, p. 136.
30. Wallerstein, *Modern World-System*, I, 152.
31. Wallerstein, *Capitalist World Economy*, p. 293.
32. Braudel, *Afterthoughts*, p. 110.

CHAPTER 2

1. Max Weber, *Economy and Society*, ed. and trans. Guenther Roth and Claus Wittich, 3 vols. (Berkeley: University of California Press, 1978), I, 4.
2. Karl Löwith, *Meaning in History* (Chicago: University of Chicago Press, 1949), pp. 8–9.
3. Hans Jonas, "The Practical Uses of Theory," *Social Research* 26 (Summer 1959), 127–129.
4. Arthur Lovejoy, *The Great Chain of Being* (New York: Harper & Row, Harper Torchbooks, 1960), p. 288.
5. Francis Bacon, "Novum Organum," in *The English Philosophers from Bacon to Mill*, ed. E. A. Burtt (New York: Modern Library, 1939), p. 26.
6. Lovejoy, *Great Chain of Being*, p. 52.
7. *Ibid.*, p. 245.
8. Quoted in Löwith, *Meaning*, pp. 52–53.
9. Quoted in *ibid.*
10. T. M. Knox, ed., *Hegel's Philosophy of Right* (Oxford: Claredon Press, 1957), p. 12.
11. This interpretation is based on Hegel's introduction to his *Philosophy of History*. See esp. R. G. Collingwood, *The Idea of History* (New York: Oxford University Press, Galaxy Book, 1956), pp. 113–120.
12. Knox, *Hegel's Philosophy of Right*, p. 11.
13. My formulation is indebted to that of Knox, in *ibid.*, p. 300.
14. Quoted in Löwith, *Meaning*, pp. 53, 55.
15. See *ibid.*, p. 59.
16. Karl Marx, "Contribution to the Critique of Hegel's *Philosophy of Right*" (1843) in Robert C. Tucker, *The Marx-Engels Reader* (New York: W. W. Norton, 1972), p. 12. I note the title and date from which the several Marx quotations are taken but use the Tucker reader for ease of contemporary reference.

17. *Ibid.,* p. 23.
18. Karl Marx and Friedrich Engels, *The German Ideology* (1845–46) in Tucker, *Marx-Engels Reader,* p. 113.
19. *Ibid.,* pp. 119–121.
20. Marx's emphasis on the long-run determination of history by the material conditions of production is his version of the objective meaning of history. Whether his distinction between a long prehistory of alienation and a future society of full self-realization can also be so characterized is another question.
21. Weber, *Economy and Society,* I, 4.
22. A careful reading of Hegel's introduction to his *Philosophy of History* reveals striking parallels between his ideas and Weber's basic definitions, although Weber clearly rejected Hegel's idea of "objective Spirit." See G. W. F. Hegel, *Vorlesungen über die Philosophie der Geschichte,* (Frankfurt: Suhrkamp Verlag, Theorie Werkausgabe, 1970), vol. 12, pp. 36–38ff.
23. Weber, *Economy and Society,* I, 7.
24. For an elaboration of this "intellectual generation" see H. Stuart Hughes, *Consciousness and Society* (New York: Alfred A. Knopf, 1958), p. 18n and passim.
25. Karl Löwith, "Max Weber und Karl Marx," in *Gesammelte Abhandlungen* (Stuttgart: W. Kohlhammer, 1960), p. 66.

CHAPTER 3

1. The quotation from Tocqueville refers to his letter of April 12, 1835, repr. in Alexis de Tocqueville, *Memoir, Letters, and Remains* (Boston: Ticknor & Fields, 1863), II, 13–14 (to M. de Corcelle); see also pp. 104–105.

   It is apparently difficult to avoid misunderstandings when this position is stated. Weber concluded his *Protestant Ethic* with the remark that "it is, of course, not my aim to substitute for a one-sided materialistic an equally one-sided spiritualistic causal interpretation of culture and of history." Nevertheless, he has been criticized time and again for having done just that—despite his continuous scholarly concern with the influences of the economy. In a similar vein, I have pointed out that the division of labor is one cause of social change in economically developing countries and that observers have been quite right in being impressed by the importance of this cause: "But with so many scholars engaged in searching for underlying structures, there is space for an inquiry which focuses attention on structures that lie more open to view. The roots of historically developed structures, of the culture and political institutions of any present-day society, reach far into the past." Those who reject this double emphasis and insist that the analysis of the long run and hence of long-lasting economic tendencies is the only "realistic" one for an understanding of society must have reasons for that insistence. With Marx (and Wallerstein?) that reason seems to have been faith in a future in which the miseries of mankind will be overcome. In the case of Braudel, the reason seems to be a feeling of resignation. On the other hand, Weber's reason as well as mine is the stubborn insistence on inquiring into the possibilities of decision making which remain available even despite the "main tendencies." Hence the emphasis on "meaningful action," on the possibilities of moral choice, on the importance of politics, of ideas and intellectuals for the determination of events. This emphasis is quite compatible with the recognition of the division of labor as an important cause of social change. Yet a learned critic of my book thought it necessary to censure me for wishing to substitute intellectual mobilization as an explanatory alternative to the division of labor. One wonders where it has been decreed that only monocausal explanations are acceptable. The two quoted sentences above are from Max Weber, *The Protestant Ethic and the Spirit of Capitalism* (New York: Charles Scribner's Sons, 1958), p. 183, and Reinhard Bendix, *Kings or People* (Berkeley: University of California Press, 1978), pp. 12–14; see also Thomas A. Brady, review of *Kings or People* in *Sixteenth Century Journal* (Winter 1980), 118.

2. Bendix, *Kings or People,* p. 198.
3. Karl Marx, *The Eighteenth Brumaire of Louis Bonaparte* (New York: International Publishers, n.d.), p. 13.

4. Quoted in Walter Ullmann, *A History of Political Thought: The Middle Ages* (Baltimore: Penguin, 1965), p. 88. See *Kings or People,* pp. 30–35.
5. Bendix, *Kings or People,* pp. 6–7.
6. E. P. Thompson, *The Making of the English Working Class* (New York: Random House, Pantheon Books, 1964), p. 12.
7. The quotation from Butterfield reads as follows: "Instead of seeing the modern world emerge as the victory of the children of light over the children of darkness in any generation, it is at least better to see it emerge as the result of a clash of wills, a result which neither party wanted or even dreamed of, a result which indeed in some cases both parties would equally have hated, but a result for the achievement of which the existence of both and the clash of both were necessary." See Herbert Butterfield, *The Whig Interpretation of History* (New York: W. W. Norton, 1965), p. 28.
8. Such differences in the level of abstraction exist in every account; it is only a question of marking them off from one another as clearly as possible. Historians deceive themselves if they believe that they only describe a sequence of events, because every description is incomplete and there is only incidental mention of what is left out. However, sociologists also deceive themselves if they believe they are able to characterize social structures by abstractions alone, because each abstraction uses everyday expressions whose many connotations also receive no mention and yet are tacitly assumed and indispensable for the sake of communication. In addition, comparative studies must also exclude materials the relevance of which is undisputed but which are sacrificed in the interest of indispensable shortcuts. For example, in *Kings or People,* pt. 2, I deal with the Reformation in England in some detail, but I then refer to it more briefly with regard to Germany and France. Or, in the case of Germany, I describe the clashes between emperor and territorial princes in order to portray the struggles in the center of Europe; then I turn with a few introductory sentences and hence quite abruptly to the history of Prussia to keep the length of the chapter within limits. There are much more troublesome omissions, as, e.g., the urban patriciate and guilds, which I neglect in

the interest of discussing church and aristocracy as counter-vailing forces of kingship, forces which ultimately contri-buted to the transition from royal to popular sovereignty. See Otto Hintze, "The Preconditions of Representative Gov-ernment in the Context of World History," in *The Historical Essays of Otto Hintze*, ed. Felix Gilbert (New York: Oxford University Press, 1975), pp. 302ff. There is probably no ideal selection of materials in comparative studies because more must be left out than can be included in order to achieve the desired breadth of comparison. It is an illusion to attempt complete coverage; the question is only whether the selection made is appropriate.

9. This exegesis of Weber's discussion is based on earlier expo-sitions. See Reinhard Bendix, *Nation-Building and Citizen-ship*, 2nd ed. (Berkeley: University of California Press, 1977), pp. 39–45, and *Kings or People*, chap. 7.

10. Quoted in J. R. Tanner, *Constitutional Conflicts of the Sev-enteenth Century* (London: Cambridge University Press, 1971), p. 265.

11. J. H. Plumb, *The Growth of Political Stability in England, 1675–1725* (Harmondsworth: Penguin Books, 1969), p. 39. My description is necessarily a simplified synopsis of this subtle study.

12. *Ibid.*, p. 78.

13. Pierre Goubert, *Louis XIV and Twenty Million Frenchmen* (New York: Random House, Vintage Books, 1970), p. 52.

14. A convenient summary is found in John Lough, *An Introduc-tion to Seventeenth Century France* (London: Longman, 1973).

15. These summaries are based on *Kings or People*, chaps. 4, 5, 12.

CHAPTER 4

1. Alexis de Tocqueville, *Democracy in America* (New York: Vintage Books, 1945), II, 189.

2. *Ibid.*, II, 188.

3. *Ibid.*, I, 5–6.

4. *Ibid.*, II, 190–191.
5. *Ibid.*, II, 194.
6. *Ibid.*, II, 195.
7. John Stuart Mill, *Principles of Political Economy* (Boston: Charles C. Little and James Brown, 1848), II, 319–320.
8. George Herbert Mead, *Movements of Thought in the Nineteenth Century* (Chicago: University of Chicago Press, 1936), p. 21.
9. *Ibid.*, p. 17.
10. Georg Friedrich Wilhelm Hegel, *Phänomenologie des Geistes* (Leipzig: Felix Mainer, 1928), pp. 143, 147. My paraphrasing attempts to convey Hegel's meaning without using his language. The relevant passages are readily accessible in *The Philosophy of Hegel*, ed. C. J. Friedrich (New York: Modern Library, 1953), pp. 399–410.
11. Tocqueville, *Democracy in America*, II, 195.
12. *Ibid.*
13. This aspect is dealt with in more detail in Chapter 5.
14. For a perceptive analysis of this development see T. H. Marshall, *Citizenship and Social Class* (Cambridge: Cambridge University Press, 1950), chap. 1. The statement in the text refers specifically to England. Social rights have been instituted in other ways, sometimes in order to withhold the establishment of civil rights as in imperial Germany.
15. An expanded statement of this point is in my article "A Study of Managerial Ideologies," *Economic Development and Cultural Change*, 5 (January 1957), 118–128.
16. The quoted phrase occurs in Burckhardt's definition of the objective of culture history, which "goes to the heart of past mankind [because] it declares what mankind *was, wanted, thought, perceived,* and *was able to do.* In this way culture history deals with what is constant, and in the end this constant appears greater and more important than the momentary, a quality appears to be greater and more instructive than an action. For actions are only the individual expressions of a certain inner capacity, which is always able to recreate these same actions. Goals and presuppositions are, therefore, as important as events." Italics added. See Jacob Burckhardt, *Griechische Kulturgeschichte*, 3 vols. (Stuttgart: Kroener, 1952), I, 6.

17. See H. Stuart Hughes, *Consciousness and Society* (New York: Alfred A. Knopf, 1958), which gives a perceptive analysis of this "generation."

18. By "ideologies" I do not refer to attitudes of the type that can be elicited in a questionnaire study, but to the constant process of formulation and reformulation by which spokesmen identified with a social group seek to articulate what they sense to be its shared understandings. I call these articulations ideologies in the specific sense of "ideas considered in the context of group action." All ideas can be analyzed from this viewpoint; hence I depart from the frequent identification of ideologies with false or misleading ideas.

19. For example, at the turn of the century American employers asserted their absolute authority over the workers, but this assertion lacked content until the bureaucratization of industry brought to the fore experts who worked out methods for the exercise of authority. Again, the tsar's assertion of authority over all the people inadvertently encouraged the peasants to appeal to him for redress of grievances. This procedure is adapted from that used by Max Weber in his sociology of religion.

20. See Karl Marx, *The Eighteenth Brumaire of Louis Bonaparte* (New York: International Publishers, n. d.), p. 13. Emphasizing the impact of cultural tradition on current ideologies is more in line with the facts than is the effort to explain those ideologies solely in terms of problems encountered by the businessman in his work. Such an interpretation leads to an elimination of ideological changes, and of differences between ideologies, because all ideologies are in this sense responses to the strains endemic in modern society. See Francis X. Sutton et al., *The American Business Creed* (Cambridge: Harvard University Press, 1956), where the change of business ideologies over time is denied and where these ideologies are explained in exactly the same terms as nationalism and anti-capitalism. See also the comments of Leland Jenks, "Business Ideologies," *Explorations of Entrepreneurial History,* 10 (October 1957), 1–7.

21. The laboring poor are asked to prove their virtue by their obedience, but they are also told that their dependence results from a natural inferiority. Similarly, if the ruling classes

do not meet their responsibility for the deserving poor, it is only because the poor who suffer are not deserving.

22. In Russia the landed aristocracy never succeeded in making itself the unavoidable intermediary between the ruler and the people, in contrast with Western Europe, where the ruler's administrative and juridical authority in effect ended at the boundaries of the estate—though this contrast merely states the end result of protracted struggles over the division of authority.

23. Lenin's statement that "the Russian is a bad worker" and his advocacy of the Taylor system of management, as well as of electrification as the road to socialism, indicate that the problems of complex industrial organizations came to the fore at once.

24. Here again I am indebted to the work of Max Weber, though more to what he did in his own studies than to what he wrote about them in his methodology. See my *Max Weber: An Intellectual Portrait* (New York: Doubleday, 1960), chap. 8.

25. See Reinhard Bendix, *Work and Authority in Industry*, 2nd ed. (Berkeley: University of California Press, 1974), p. 251. To avoid a possible misunderstanding, I add that this assertion is in my judgment compatible with the endeavor to put managerial decision making on a more scientific basis. The substitution of machine methods for manual operations is obviously an ongoing process which has greatly curtailed the areas of possible discretion, although machine methods also create new opportunities for discretionary judgments. But though these methods and organizational manipulations may curtail and reallocate the areas in which discretion is possible or desired, and may in this way achieve greater efficiency, they cannot, I believe, eliminate discretion.

26. Hence they will do so even for the purpose of achieving the objective of the party itself. See Joseph Berliner, *Factory and Manager in the USSR* (Cambridge: Harvard University Press, 1957), which documents that the most successful Soviet managers use the systematic subversion of authoritative commands for the purpose of realizing the ends of these commands, as well as for their personal convenience. This fact suggests that "good faith" can be inculcated in many ways,

even by the systematic distrust of all subordinates—provided of course that the distrust has a higher rationale, such as the utopian and nationalist ideology of Russian Communism.

27. For a more generalized treatment of this approach to totalitarianism, see Reinhard Bendix, *Nation-Building and Citizenship*, 2nd ed. (Berkeley: University of California Press, 1977), chap. 5.
28. This theme is elaborated in Joseph Schumpeter, *Capitalism, Socialism and Democracy* (New York: Harper, 1950 [Torchbook ed., 1962]).

CHAPTER 5

1. See the analysis of these dominant ideas in the context of social and intellectual history in Otto Brunner, *Adeliges Landleben und Europäischer Geist* (Salzburg: Otto Mueller, 1949). For a behavioristic rather than a theoretical analysis of the social contract, cf. my book *Nation-Building and Citizenship*, 2nd ed. (Berkeley: University of California Press, 1977), pp. 86–89, and Barrington Moore, *Injustice: The Social Bases of Obedience and Revolt* (New York: M. W. Sharpe, 1978), e.g., pp. 203, 455–457.
2. See the illuminating material in Werner Danckert, *Unehrliche Leute: Die Verfemten Berufe* (Bern: Francke Verlag, 1979).
3. Lorenz von Stein, "Der Begriff der Arbeit und die Prinzipien des Arbeitslohns in ihrem Verhältnis zum Sozialismus und Kommunismus," *Zeitschrift für die gesamte Sozialwissenschaft*, III (1846), 263.
4. John Stuart Mill, *Principles of Political Economy*, 2 vols. (Boston: Charles C. Little and James Brown, 1848), II, 322–323.
5. Karl Marx, *Frühe Schriften*, vol. II: *Das Elend der Philosophie*, ed. H. J. Lieber and Peter Furth (Darmstadt: Wissenschaftliche Buchgesellschaft, 1975), pp. 809–810.
6. A survey of the concept "alienation" in the context of the history of ideas is contained in Joachim Israel, *Alienation: From Marx to Modern Sociology* (Atlantic Highlands, N. J.: Humanities Press, 1979).

7. See Engels' letter to Marx of October 7, 1858, in Karl Marx and Friedrich Engels, *Ausgewählte Briefe* (Berlin: Dietz Verlag, 1953), pp. 131–132.

8. This brief summary is based on earlier writings on Russian social history. Compare Reinhard Bendix, *Work and Authority in Industry*, 2nd ed. (Berkeley: University of California Press, 1974), chap. 3, and *Kings or People* (Berkeley: University of California Press, 1978), chap. 13.

9. Quoted in Philip Pomper, *Peter Lavrov and the Russian Revolution* (Chicago: University of Chicago Press, 1972), p. 102.

10. Karl Marx, *The Holy Family* (1845), quoted in Robert C. Tucker, ed., *The Marx-Engels Reader* (New York: W. W. Norton, 1972), pp. 105–106.

11. Karl Marx and Friedrich Engels, *The Communist Manifesto* (1848) repr. in Tucker, *Marx-Engels Reader*, pp. 345–346.

12. Karl Marx, preface to the 1st. ed. of *Capital*, repr. in Tucker, *Marx-Engels Reader*, p. 193.

13. See the following statement from a speech by the Chartist leader Hartwell, delivered in 1837: "It seems to me to be an anomaly that in a country where the arts and sciences have been raised to such height, chiefly by the industry, skill and labours of the artisan . . . only one adult male in seven should have a vote, that in such a country the working classes should be excluded from the pale of political life." Quoted in M. Beer, *A History of British Socialism* (London: Allen & Unwin, 1948), II, 25–26. It is instructive to contrast this statement with that by the Italian nationalist leader Mazzini: "Without Country you have neither name, token, voice, nor rights. . . . Do not beguile yourselves with the hope of emancipation from unjust social conditions if you do not first conquer a Country for yourselves. . . . Do not be led away by the idea of improving your material conditions without first solving the national question. . . . Today you are not the working class of Italy; you are only fractions of that class. . . . Your emancipation can have no practical beginning until a National Government [is founded]." See Joseph Mazzini, *The Duties of Man and Other Essays* (New York: E. P. Dutton, 1912), pp. 53–54.

14. This viewpoint differs from Marxism, which treats politics

and government as variables dependent upon the changing organization of production, without coming to grips either with the relative autonomy of governmental actions or the continuous existence of national political communities. It also differs from the sociological approach to politics and formal institutions which construes the first as a mere by-product of interactions among individuals and the second as the "outward shell" inside which these interactions provide the clue to a realistic understanding of social life. Compare the critical analysis of this reductionism in Sheldon Wolin, *Politics and Vision* (Boston: Little, Brown, 1960), chaps. 9, 10.

15. See in this respect Friedrich Engels' expression of disgust with the ingrained "respectability" of English workers and their leaders in his letter to Sorge of December 7, 1889 in Marx, Engels, *Ausgewählte Briefe,* 495.

16. The perspective presented here has been developed by some of my former students. The study by Guenther Roth entitled *The Social Democrats in Imperial Germany* (New York: Bedminster Press, 1963) discusses the problem under the heading "Working-Class Isolation and Negative Integration." See also Gaston Rimlinger, "The Legitimation of Protest: A Comparative Study in Labor History," *Comparative Studies in Society and History* 2 (April 1960), 329–343, and "Social Security, Incentives and Controls in the U.S. and the USSR," *Comparative Studies in Society and History* 4 (November 1961), 104–124.

CHAPTER 6

1. Francis Bacon, *Novum Organum,* in *The English Philosophers from Bacon to Mill,* ed. E. A. Burtt, (New York: Modern Library, 1939), p. 85.

2. Carlo Cipolla, *Guns and Sails in the Early Phase of European Expansion* (London: Collins, 1965).

3. See Elizabeth Eisenstein, *The Printing Press as an Agent of Change* (New York: Columbia University Press, 1980) for a detailed examination of the evidence.

4. A. M. Carr-Saunders and P. A. Wilson, *The Professions* (London: Frank Cass, 1964).

CHAPTER 6 (continued)

5. Raymond Williams, *The Long Revolution* (London: Chatto & Windus, 1961).
6. Wilhelm Riehl, *Die bürgerliche Gesellschaft* (Stuttgart: Cotta, 1930), pp. 312ff.
7. Michael Walzer, *The Revolution of the Saints* (New York: Athenaeum, 1970).
8. W. R. Prest, *The Inns of Court under Elizabeth and the Early Stuarts* (London: Longman, 1972).
9. P. Zagorin, *The Court and the Country, The Beginnings of the English Revolution* (New York: Athenaeum, 1971).
10. G. Wiener, "The Beleaguered Isle. A Study of Elizabethan and Early Jacobean Anti-Catholicism," *Past and Present*, Nr. 51 (1971), pp. 27–62.
11. Pierre Goubert, *Louis XIV and Twenty Million Frenchmen* (New York: Random House, 1970).
12. Reinhard Bendix, *Kings or People* (Berkeley: University of California Press, 1978), pp. 339–350.
13. See *ibid.*, chap. 8, and the earlier discussion in Reinhard Bendix, "Tradition and Modernity Reconsidered," in *Nation-Building and Citizenship* (Berkeley: University of California Press, 1977), pp. 361–434.
14. The concept of "reference societies" is modeled after Max Weber's idea of social action as well as the idea of "reference group" of Robert K. Merton. See Robert K. Merton, *Social Theory and Social Structure* (Glencoe: The Free Press, 1957), pp. 225–386. "Demonstration effect" is a familiar category in economics.
15. Alexander Gerschenkron, *Economic Backwardness in Historical Perspective* (New York: Praeger, 1965).
16. Klaus Epstein, *The Genesis of German Conservatism* (Princeton: Princeton University Press, 1966), pp. 391ff.
17. Marvin Zonis, "Islam," *University of Chicago Magazine* (September 1980), p. 12.
18. Quoted by Isaiah Berlin in his introduction to Franco Venturi, *Roots of Revolution* (New York: Grosset & Dunlop, 1966), p. xx.

19. See Clifford Geertz, "The Integrative Revolution," in Clifford Geertz, ed., *Old Societies and New States* (Glencoe: The Free Press, 1963), pp. 105–157, and Clifford Geertz, "The Judging of Nations," in *Europäisches Archiv für Soziologie*, vol. 18 (1977), pp. 245–261.
20. Michael Hechter, *Internal Colonialism* (Berkeley: University of California Press, 1977).
21. D. M. Earl, *Emperor and Nation in Japan* (Seattle: University of Washington Press, 1964).
22. Quoted in Adam Yarmolinsky, *Road to Revolution* (New York: Collier Books, Macmillan Co., 1962), p. 73.

Designer: Janet Wood
Compositor: Huron Valley Graphics
Text: 10/12 Times Roman
Display: Times Roman Italic
Printer: Vail-Ballou Press
Binder: Vail-Ballou Press